THE PIT

THE TRUE CRIME STORY OF SIX WOMEN, ONE MONSTER, AND THE NIGHTMARE BELOW

RYAN GREEN

For Helen, Harvey, Frankie and Dougie

Disclaimer

This book is about real people committing real crimes. The story has been constructed by facts but some of the scenes, dialogue and characters have been fictionalised.

Polite Note to the Reader

This book is written in British English except where fidelity to other languages or accents are appropriate. Some words and phrases may differ from US English.

Copyright © Ryan Green 2025

All rights reserved

ISBN: 9798283670935

YOUR FREE BOOK IS WAITING

From bestselling author Ryan Green

There is a man who is officially classed as **"Britain's most dangerous prisoner"**

The man's name is Robert Maudsley, and his crimes earned him the nickname **"Hannibal the Cannibal"**

This free book is an exploration of his story...

"Ryan brings the horrifying details to life. I can't wait to read more by this author!"

Get a free copy of **Robert Maudsley: Hannibal the Cannibal** when you sign up to join my Reader's Group.

www.ryangreenbooks.com/free-book

CONTENTS

What Lies Beneath 7
East Lake 13
One Boy's War 29
The House That God Built 50
Down in the Dark Place 63
What Is Owed 76
The Pit 90
Dog Food 108
Bad Investment 118
Want More? 126
Every Review Helps 127
About Ryan Green 128
More Books by Ryan Green 129
Free True Crime Audiobook 134

What Lies Beneath

Her knight in shining armor had just ridden in and she didn't even know it. All around them, the other in-patients were scattered with their visitors. On overstuffed sofas layered over with plastic to prevent the worst of the stains, mommies and daddies were giving their little girls and boys cuddles, but not her. Her mommy and daddy didn't come around anymore. Left her here to rot. Forgot all about her, once a year for Christmas and then nothing more. She embarrassed them. She knew she did. Even if she couldn't spell the word. They looked at her and their eyes got sad. Even when they were smiling as widely as they could, their eyes were sad.

Her knight though, his eyes weren't sad. They were bright and shiny, and his smile made it all the way up to them, and he was saying things to her, but she hadn't heard them because there was too much noise. Too many people speaking all at once. This was meant to be a quiet room, but the visitors didn't know that and they talked very loudly. So loud it made her want to cover her ears so she wouldn't hear anything, but then she wouldn't be able to hear what her knight was saying.

Her knight wasn't her knight yet. He was a stranger. Stranger danger. Somebody she had never seen before. She didn't trust people she'd never seen before. Didn't trust most people she had seen before either. Not after they made her go to bed early or watched her use the toilet or bullied her for not knowing how to play their card games or… He was still talking and she was missing it all.

"I'm a friend."

That she understood, those were the kind of words she used. Friend. She had a friend once but he got moved to somewhere else. His mommy and daddy hadn't paid the bills so he was moved to the state hospital and that meant that they couldn't see each other anymore or swap puddings when they got the kind that they didn't like as much. He was gone now, and that warm little feeling she got in her tummy when he held her hand was gone, too. She feared she would never see him again, just like grandpa and grandma, but she knew her grandparents had gone somewhere you could never come back from while her friend might come back someday. Except she thought that her friend's mommy and daddy had gone to that place you couldn't come back from too, so they would never pay their bills, so he'd never come back either.

"I'm a friend of your sister."

Her sister. She had a sister. Big sis. Clever girl. She wished she was as clever as her big sister. Her big sister was so clever she didn't have to go to a place like this. They let her stay outside in the big world with the big boys and girls. She was so lucky. She got to go nap when she wanted to and eat food she liked and she didn't have to go to where she was told to go all the time. She could do anything because she was so smart. When she was little, she had been here, or in whatever place they were in before here, with the younger ones who couldn't live in the outside world. But then they had gotten bigger and her sister had gotten smarter and they had said she could go outside and be with mommy and daddy. When she came back, she was wearing different clothes every time.

This man wasn't really a stranger. He was a friend of her big sister. Her big sister was so clever, there was no way that she would be friends with a stranger. She knew about stranger danger too, so if this was a stranger then her sister would never have been friends with him.

What if he was lying? There were people here who said they were her friends, but they weren't. They came into her room at night. They pushed her when she was in line for lunch. They stole pieces of the puzzles and hid them so she couldn't solve them and then they called her a dumb-dumb even though it wasn't her fault that the pieces were gone. It was their fault for taking the pieces but when she tried to tell the nurses, they just looked at her with sad eyes and pretended that they believed her, but she knew they also thought she was just a dumb-dumb. It wasn't fair. She wasn't a dumb-dumb. She wasn't. They were liars. What if this man was a liar too?

As if he had heard her inner thoughts, the man said, "If you get up and walk over to the window there and look outside, you can see your sister. She's sitting in the front seat of my car. And she is waiting for you to go out and see her. Would you like to go see her?"

He'd changed the way he was speaking to her. He was talking slower. Using easier words. Making sure she was understanding him before saying something else, just like her sister used to do. Like her mommy and daddy never got used to doing. They were always like little bees, buzzing about too fast for her to catch them. Always busy. Too busy to slow down for her. That was good. Him slowing down. Not mommy and daddy being so busy.

When he went slow she didn't miss so much, even though it was still too noisy in here. She got back to her feet, still keeping her eyes on him, and walked over to the window. If her sister was there, then he wasn't a liar. If her sister was there, she could wave and say, "Hello sister. I have missed you, sister. I have missed you for so long. I have missed you since mommy and daddy brought you at Christmas time."

Out there in the front of the car, she could see her sister. Her sister waved to her, and she waved back. The nurses started heading over in case she was going to be trouble, but she wasn't. She definitely wasn't going to be trouble. The man she didn't know, the friend of her sister, waved to the nurses and they decided that everything was okay. She didn't know how he did that, but he did, and now everything was easier. If they knew her sister was out there, it would have been fine for her to go to the window and wave, but if her sister wasn't there, she might have been making trouble and they didn't like that at all. Not one bit. You got put on punishment if you made trouble. They would have just had to look to see her sister, but they wouldn't have bothered, they would have asked her questions, and it was when she was trying to explain that there would have been trouble. She knew what she wanted them to know, and she said words she thought would make sense, but nobody ever seemed to understand. They treated her like she was a naughty little baby. But she wasn't. She was more than twenty years old. She had counted. And they had only put one candle on her cake. And even if she wasn't more than twenty years old, the doctor had said that she was as smart as any five-year-old, so they still shouldn't have treated her like a baby. If the doctor was right, and he was very clever, then they should have tried harder, they should have listened to her and understood what she was trying to tell them, but they never did. They always looked bored and had sad eyes. They always wanted to stop talking to her right away even when they were the ones who had started talking to her.

Ambling back over to the table with the man she didn't know was her knight in shining armour, she sat back down and looked at him. He was a white man, and mommy and daddy weren't, and her sister wasn't, and they didn't have many friends who were white men back when they still came around, but this man was white, with his hair all slicked back and his big smile with little thin lips. He was smiling at her, not like the doctors did when she was being good, or like the nurses did when they got to tell her off for being trouble, but like something else. Something new. Like her sister did sometimes. Like he could be her friend, the way he was her sister's friend.

'Now you know I'm your sister's friend, and she is here, I wondered if you might like to go outside with us, for a while?'

That was silly. That didn't make any sense. Go outside? She wasn't allowed out into the world. It was too big and bad and scary for her. She wasn't smart enough. She would be in big trouble if she went outside. Everyone said so. She had to stay inside where it was safe, and they'd take care of her. Who would take care of her if she went outside? Who would give her food, dress her, and make sure she went to the toilet and did all the things she needed to do but didn't know how to do for herself? She wasn't allowed. He had to know that.

And somehow, he did, he saw the frown on her face, and he explained. 'I asked the nice people here if we could take you out for a little trip and bring you back, and they said that as long as I took care of you, that would be A-okay with them. I got a special pass for you.'

That was too many words, too many abstract ideas, her frown deepened as she tried to pick through them. "If you want to go outside with me, and see your sister, that is allowed, as long as you stay with me."

He laid his hand on the table in between them, palm up, fingers curled just a little. He was offering it to her. Since her friend had left, nobody had touched her except when they were scrubbing her in the shower, and that wasn't the same. That wasn't a nice touch, that was a rough one, that was all business. All business. Nobody had held her hand since her friend, or her sister. This man was offering her the first kindness she had experienced in a long while. Tentatively, unsure, she reached out towards it, expecting him to jerk it back at any moment, the way the nurses and doctors sometimes did if she tried to touch them.

But he didn't move. He sat completely still, with his hand held out, and when she put her hand on top of it, he closed his fingers around it, and it was warm and dry and nice. He was smiling at her, holding her hand, and looking at her like he was happy to be looking at her. Nobody was ever happy to look at her. Not ever.

"Go out?" She managed to mumble after far too long – lost in the glory of the sensation. The brief spark of light in the vast void of loneliness that consumed her every waking moment had distracted her, but the man didn't look mad that she'd been lost in thought. He was still smiling.

"That's right," He nodded eagerly, "You and me and your sister, we're going to take a little trip. Go see some sights. Does that sound good to you?"

"Sounds good." She repeated back to him.

"Well alright then." He took her by the hand, and drew her up to standing, like she was a princess at a ball, being asked to dance.

That was the last solid memory she had to hang onto. Her knight in shining armor, rescuing her from the bad place, going to her room and getting her dressed, taking her out past the desk through the locked doors, signing the paper that made it so she could leave. It was all a blur. After so long with nothing happening in her life, too much was happening and it was all flying by. She was holding his hand again, being led around by it. He was smiling at her, smiling at everyone, even when they weren't smiling back. And then she was waving goodbye, and he was calling back one last reassurance. "Don't you worry. I'm going to take real good care of her."

East Lake

On November 22, 1943, Michael and Ellen Heidnik welcomed their firstborn son into the world. Gary was perfect – with his mother's dark wavy hair and his father's piercing blue eyes, they felt like he had gotten the best of both of them. Not that there was a lot of good for either one of them to give. Both were functional alcoholics by the time of his birth, and both suffered from severe bouts of depression and other emotional instabilities that would come to define their lives and their marriage. Thanks to those instabilities their marriage was tempestuous, to put it lightly, with constant passionate fights devolving into equally passionate apologies that would eventually culminate in his brother Terry being born just a short while after him.

They lived a fairly normal life in the East Lake suburb of Cleveland, Ohio. Neither child was particularly notable in their early years, nor did they have much interaction with people outside of their immediate family. It wasn't so much that the Heidnik parents were insular, as that they just had more pressing matters to attend to within the family that distracted them from what was going on outside of it. Michael had drinking buddies, Ellen had the church, but neither had much else except for each other. Perhaps that is why they clung to each other for so long despite the fact that they were blatantly incompatible. Adding fuel to the familial disharmony was the fact that their respective mental illnesses seemed to do little more than exacerbate the issues of their partner. The relentless cycle of vicious fights followed by passionate reconciliations went on for some time before they finally began to pull apart. Each of them began having affairs outside of the marriage in an attempt to find the kind of affection and stability they were unable to offer each other. They each found what they were looking for so easily that it made all the years they had been struggling to make their marriage work look even more foolish. They did not, by any stretch of the imagination, part amicably. They couldn't even affably share a meal together, so the idea that they could go through a divorce without bitter arguments and harsh recriminations was laughable. They did, however, eventually make it through the process.

Ellen took the children when she departed. Somewhere in the midst of the divorce proceedings, the boys had become a trophy that both sides wanted to claim, whether they actually wanted to raise the kids or not, and as such it was with an air of triumph that she and the children departed from their family home with all their belongings stowed away in the back of a pickup truck. It had been readily apparent to everyone that Michael would have been an unsuitable single parent and that he would have struggled greatly with raising the two boys by himself while also trying to hold down a full-time job. Not only that, there was the catalogue of abuse claims being made against Michael by his wife that fell strictly into the "he said, she said" category. Such accusations couldn't be used as hard evidence during the divorce proceedings but were more than enough to colour everyone's opinion of Michael and make it seem crystal clear that the boys would not be safe if placed in his tender loving care. When Ellen had produced the wooden toy aeroplane that Gary had been beaten with when his father discovered that he'd committed the unpardonable sin of wetting the bed, all argument regarding who should be the boys' primary carer fizzled out quite rapidly.

The court, which served as the children's advocate during the divorce proceedings, made its decisions based on what was believed to be in the best interests of the children rather than what best suited the adults involved. While Ellen was far from the most grounded and sensible of single mothers she was, nonetheless, a better option than her soon-to-be ex-husband. There was, of course, a massive scandal over a divorce occurring in the sleepy suburb of East Lake in the year 1946. The Second World War had only just ended the previous year and the country was enjoying the post-war boom that would eventually typify the 1950s. It was an era of prosperity and growth and was characterized by the "baby boom" generation, strong family values and the development of suburban communities. Ellen was considered some sort of non-conformist deviant for her decision not to stay and suffer more of Michael's abuse and some sort of anti-family monster for taking her boys away from their father and heading out of town so that their paths could never again cross.

In truth, however, it was less of a cruelty and more of a necessity. With stigma clinging to her after the divorce, her life and that of the kids would have been ruined if she'd stuck around. Only in a new place could they have a fresh start.

She would remarry before the boys were old enough to go to school, and from all reports, while her new marriage was by no means happy, it was certainly a good deal more stable than her previous one. The boys were not treated as her new husband's own, but they were treated with a degree of kindness and respect that would have been atypical for the time period, so it was something of a surprise that the boys remained as unhappy as they had ever been. It was almost as if there were some sort of genetic component to the malaise that followed them throughout their lives rather than the circumstances in which they found themselves.

Just as the boys didn't seem to change too much, so too was the case with Ellen. It would have been reasonable to assume that her alcoholism was a reaction to living in an abusive household with someone else who indulged heavily, but the sad truth was that she drank as a means of self-medication, to help her deal with her own mental health issues. This meant that fleeing all of her problems and starting her life over wasn't very effective, given that most of her problems were inescapably packed and ready to go inside her own head.

While they had been staying with their father, the boys had an obvious antagonist, but now that their mother was their primary caregiver, the flaws in her parenting became a good deal more obvious.

The Heidnik boys started school while living with their mother, and their lack of socialization from an early age became readily apparent. Neither one of them fit in terribly well at school, but while Terry had the good sense to keep his head down and let the insults come as he became accustomed to his new environment, Gary went on the offensive, picking fights and demanding that he be left alone, which had the opposite of the desired effect, as it showed the bullies how easy it was to elicit a reaction from him.

This never really came to anything for the first year or so of schooling, when they were too young for anything truly upsetting to happen, but that all changed in a single, unfortunate moment.

Like most boys that did not care for their home life, Gary and Terry spent a great deal of their time outdoors, exploring their neighbourhood and getting into all manner of the usual mischief typical of little boys. For instance, they would often climb trees in their neighbourhood, particularly when it was long past time for them to be home for supper and they were trying to stay out of their mother's sight as she called for them. It was during one such time, as the boys tried to escape the onerous duty of returning home before dinner was ruined, that Gary scrambled up a tree ahead of his brother, reached for the next branch, missed, and fell straight back down onto the hard-packed earth – landing directly on his head. He was knocked unconscious, and Terry initially believed that his brother was dead. Instead of running to fetch help, he gave in to panicking and weeping. Eventually, Gary began to convulse, and it became apparent that he was, in fact, still alive. Obviously, the damage to his brain from the fall was significant enough to knock Gary out and cause a seizure, but it was impossible to know the exact extent of the damage done or how it might later affect the boy. Finally deciding he needed some help, Terry ran home to get his mother and the two of them managed to manhandle Gary home and into his bed. Before long, the convulsions stopped and Gary lay as motionless as if a bullet had left him for dead. He was breathing and his heart still beat, but beyond that, there was no sign that he was still alive at all.

Their mother was flung into the throes of grief and horror. She broke down at the thought that one of her beautiful boys was going to die. She panicked about the cost of a funeral. She realized with sinking dread that the death of one boy might result in her being labelled as an unfit parent allowing her accursed ex-husband to claim custody of Terry. She clung to Gary's hand. She wept. She drank. She prayed, one of her most common refuges from harsh reality. But through all of her crises, both real and imagined, the one thing that did not seem to occur to her was that she should call a doctor. All night she sat by his bedside going through fits of hysterics, dropping to her knees in prayer and frantically trying to calculate how she might somehow manage to blame this deadly debacle on her husband's actions so that Terry couldn't be snatched from her. This went on until deep in the early hours of the morning when Gary's eyes opened.

It was the miracle they'd been praying for. And it was, indeed, miraculous that Gary had survived his head injury more or less unscathed in spite of receiving no medical care for it. He could not speak initially, nor did he seem to have full control of his bodily functions anymore. When he was being spoon-fed soup, it would often run down his chin because he failed to swallow it. When he needed to use the bathroom, his ability to communicate that need, or his awareness that he needed to go, often failed, resulting in him lying in his own filth until his mother returned to change him. He could not move around on his own, he could not function whatsoever for days, but gradually, he slowly got back to some semblance of his normal self again. He would still falter sometimes. The control of his body was impacted by the injury, but for the most part, he was a normal boy again, at least physically.

The effect that the injury had on his mind was even more subtle. It is difficult, if not impossible, to say whether his subsequent change in personality was a result of the emotional trauma that he had suffered from his near-death experience or the result of actual physical damage having been done to the structures of his brain. He had never been the most outgoing, but there had been moments of warmth. But after his journey through the valley of the shadow of death, he became withdrawn, standoffish, and far less amenable to follow the lead of others. Where before he had laughed and smiled and enjoyed the company of others, he now kept mostly to himself, rarely engaging with anyone, even Terry, who he had always been so close to.

There was another unexpected side-effect of his injury that wouldn't become obvious to him until he was recovered enough to go back to school. The injury had broken some of the bones of his skull, and they had knitted back together incorrectly. The shape of his head was changed, deformed. The other students were quick to notice this and picked on him for it. They called him "football head" which, if you are familiar with the elongated shape of an American football, served as an apt enough description for how his skull had been reshaped.

Where the Gary of before would have taken that good-natured ribbing and given as good as he got, this new Gary endured the insults in seething silence. He had always been an intelligent boy, scoring well on every test and never struggling with his schoolwork, and while the odd moments of confusion crept into him now when he tried to draw on memories and found them absent, overall he remained much smarter than the children around him. Before, this had not caused him any social problems because of his good nature and aptitude for diffusing uncomfortable situations, but now he fixated on it. It was the difference between him and all these other children. They mocked him for an injury that could have befallen any one of them, when all the while, he was better than them. He was their superior. Like the Tarzan stories he'd read, he was a man raised among apes.

The other children gradually learned to avoid Gary, and he seemed to relish avoiding them in turn, refusing to even make eye contact with them unless circumstances forced him to. His intelligence, which had always been tempered by empathy, now became gross arrogance. A new girl, who had seen his isolation approached him in class one morning to ask if he'd gotten the homework done, and he launched into an egotistical rant about how she was not worthy to speak with him. This exacerbated his isolation, as any trace of pity that anyone might have felt towards him fully evaporated.

But while he was an unpleasant nuisance at school, that was nothing compared to his behaviour at home. His newfound sense of superiority extended to his mother as well, and while he could seek solitude from his classmates, there was no escaping from her. Without the empathy that had once held him back, he was now more than happy to tell her exactly what he thought of her, of her parenting, and of just how useless she was as a mother. Given that she was already extremely emotionally unbalanced, this did not serve to foster a very convivial atmosphere in the home. When she wasn't hysterically sobbing, she was screaming at him, and when he lashed back, proving how ineffective talking to him like that was, she had no alternative approach. It isn't entirely fair to say that he outclassed her intellectually, but there was a degree of truth to his assessment that he was capable of making better decisions than she. She had, after all, made numerous critical errors several times throughout his life that had resulted in extended unhappy periods in their shared history. Her parenting mistakes ranged from all the years she'd made excuses for her abusive ex-husband to failing to seek medical treatment for a child that had been knocked unconscious by a head injury, and everything in between. He blamed her for most of his own unhappiness, and he did not shy away from explaining to her in excruciating detail all the ways that she'd failed as a mother whenever he had the opportunity to do so.

This blossomed from a two-way street of emotional abuse into all-out warfare between the two of them, with both trying their best to devastate the other as much as possible. Whatever tentative authority Ellen had held over Gary was now long lost, and he did whatever he pleased, coming and going from the house freely, and daring her to try and stop him. The few times there had been physical altercations, they had not ended well for Ellen. She may have been bigger and stronger than her preteen son, but he was infinitely more vicious and willing to do her harm. In a bout of passion, she might slap him, but without her emotions overpowering her sense of reason, she didn't want to hurt him. He did not feel the same way. If anything, he seemed to relish the opportunity to hurt her, as if it was payback for everything that she had done that had steered their lives to this point.

This went on for far longer than it ever should have, before Ellen finally made the last bad decision affecting Gary's life that she would ever make. She was incapable of instilling discipline in him, and she had come to accept that. He was going to run all over her, doing whatever he pleased, and his whole life, and hers, were going to be ruined as a result. What luck that she had an alternative option. A second household where Gary and his brother could be raised, where she would no longer have to bear the brunt of his abuse, and she could get back to enjoying life with her new partner without the fear of coming home to find Gary had burned the house down out of spite.

At the ripe old age of seven, Gary was sent back to his father in East Lake. In the family home that Gary and Terry had been raised in from birth, Michael Heidnik had started over. He had a new wife, a new life, and the arrival of these two troublemaking boys was not going to be allowed to disrupt all of that.

Gary was as defiant with his father as he'd ever been with his mother, coming into the new household with the same superior attitude that had gotten him kicked out of the last one. It would not last long. The part of the equation that had been missing when he lived with his mother were the consequences of his actions. He had done what he wanted, when he wanted, without there being any sort of notable repercussions. That would not be the case in his father's house. Quite the opposite, in fact. Before he could even start to raise hell, hell was brought down upon them. Terry had picked up on his older brother's truculent attitude and had begun talking back to adults in much the same way that Gary did. But while Gary had a prodigy's intellect to back it up, to outwit them and redirect them, all that Terry had was pure defiance. Within hours of arriving at their father's house, he had talked back to Michael and been slapped so hard that his ear began to bleed. It would not be until later in life that the boys would realize that this single brutal blow had burst Terry's eardrum.

There would be no physically overpowering Michael, and he was too stubborn to be talked into anything, either. It didn't matter how well-presented Gary's arguments might have been if his father wasn't listening and didn't care about anything that the boy had to say. They were his sons, so they would be fed, they would live under his roof, and they would obey his every command. Any attempt to circumvent that fact of their new lives would be punished swiftly and severely.

It might seem that given his defiance and opposition to his mother, Gary might have reacted poorly to this kind of treatment, and of course, when he was punished violently for acting out, he did respond poorly. He hated his father, hated his life, hated everything. But aside from those moments, the solid structure and regimented routine of life in his father's house actually seemed to help him a lot. While living with his mother, everything had been chaotic, and when he had lost control over his own mind and it began to run wild, there was no way to bring it back under control even if he had wanted to. The structure of a disciplined household benefited Gary immensely. It didn't entirely deal with the personality problems that he'd developed since his fall, but it gave him a blueprint for the rest of his life that he could build upon.

When he began attending school in East Lake, there were none of the outspoken comments, nor did he denigrate the intelligence of the teachers or his classmates. He was considered a polite boy because he held himself entirely aloof, speaking only when spoken to, and only when necessary. He was not well-liked by the other students, but neither was he picked on in the way that he had been in his previous school. He was still excessively proud of his own achievements and contemptuous of others, but he had learned not to communicate that contempt, lest his father hear about his bad behaviour and unpleasant consequences would follow.

Terry was not so quick to adapt to the new normal. He was younger, and he didn't have the incisive intellect that Gary had used to immediately assess their new situation. Sometimes he would get upset, sometimes he'd talk out of turn, or forget to do something that was his duty to attend to, or sometimes he'd just piss their dad off by existing. They were both young, and with that youth, there came a degree of clumsiness. Dropping things was a mortal sin under Michael's watch. Every time he heard something drop in his house, whether it be one of the plates that the kids were using to set the table, a broom being dropped in the midst of sweeping the house, or even a toy being fumbled in their room where they hid from him, it would set Michael off. How he convinced himself that every object being dropped was a personal affront to him was unclear, but what was clear was that each time the children dropped something, whichever one was responsible would receive a solid thrashing, and if neither one of them would admit to being the guilty party, both of them would be beaten.

It would have been an excellent way to drive a wedge between the two boys, making them turn on each other, siding with their father against the other until one of them received the full burden of punishment, but instead, it became a rallying point for their friendship. Gary was always assumed to be the troublemaker, and while he wouldn't go out of his way to lay claim to his brother's beatings, neither did he deny his guilt, even when he wasn't guilty of the terrible crime of which he was being accused. He bore the brunt of the attacks, and his brother bore witness to his courage, galvanizing the pair of them in their bond.

Eventually, they would come to fear picking anything up, or bumping into anything; they crept carefully through the house, with their hands tucked together behind their backs so that they would not accidentally touch anything. They stopped playing with their toys, they set the table with calculated and precise movements, one plate at a time, laying everything down on the table before carefully placing it in its assigned spot. The only time that they would pick anything up at all was when it related to one of their chores, and it was always with a ridiculous amount of care.

The first time that Gary walked into a room and found his brother unconscious and bleeding on the floor was also the last time. He would take the time, as he nursed Terry back to health, to explain their new situation to him in depth. He would explain that they were prisoners in Michael's house, that he was their warden and that nobody was coming to save them. They would get out when they were old enough to leave and live on their own, but until then, this hell was their home, and they'd have to endure it. Reasoning with their father might have been impossible, given the man's foul temper, but reasoning with little Terry was the easiest thing that Gary had ever done. His brother was already desperate for guidance, ready to believe anything his big brother said to him. When Gary laid out a new pattern for his world to fit into, with them as the heroes, their father as the monster, and everything they did as steps to surviving him, he absorbed it instantly and made it a part of his worldview. He was not laid up in bed for long. After a day, he was up and about again, doing his chores in sullen silence as bruises blossomed all over his face. There were no after-effects of his concussion the way that there had been for Gary, other than him becoming increasingly well-behaved.

The after-effects of Gary's own injury, however, still haunted him. He had headaches intermittently. Not so often that it was cause for alarm, but certainly more often than was normal. He had bouts of nausea at unexpected times. While such fluctuations in awareness were likely what would later become known as absence seizures, there is no way to be sure. We do know that he didn't have full-on grand mal seizures as often afflict people with a history of significant head injuries and he did have a more sporadic control over his body than he had before. He lost his edge in sports, and he often lost his place while reading. Generally speaking, Gary's abilities were just a little diminished from what he'd been capable of before. In the daytime, these little discrepancies went overlooked. It could be passed off as a distraction, momentary and fleeting. But at night, when he lost control of his body, there were consequences. As a small child left in the care of his father, Gary had been beaten regularly for the grievous sin of wetting the bed. Once away from his father, he had soon recovered from that habit, but after his brain injury, it had resurfaced intermittently while they were still staying with their mother. Now it happened to him with a terrible regularity. Whether it was a result of these blips in the control of his bodily functions, or as a result of the deep-seated trauma of all the past beatings is difficult to say, but try as he might, there seemed to be nothing that he could do to prevent himself from wetting the bed night after night.

Assuming that it was an involuntary reaction resulting from his injury, his father's reaction paints him as something of an idiot, but Michael didn't seem to acknowledge that there had been any injury or that anything about Gary had changed in any way. To acknowledge that would be to acknowledge that there was something unusual about him, about their house, about their life. It would tacitly acknowledge that it wasn't normal for a kid that age to have massive head trauma, or be knocked unconscious, or come to school covered in bruises. In all likelihood, the return to his childhood home and the resumption of the pitiless shaming and brutal beatings surrounding the bedwetting behaviour were the actual culprits.

To punish him with a simple beating was not enough for Michael. He didn't just want the boy hurt, he was a tough kid who'd survived worse than Michael was willing to dole out. He wanted the boy to be too mortified to ever even consider making that kind of mess again, pissing all over his house like he was a damn dog. When the boy pissed all over his sheets, they weren't going to be squirreled away so his shame could be hidden. Michael had grander plans. He made the boy strip the bed and hang the sheets out to dry. Right out of his own window. So that all the neigbours could look up and see exactly what that boy had done. Gary would spend the whole day with his ears cocked, thinking that every little giggle was about him pissing himself. He'd go to school smelling of it, and he'd sleep in it again at night unless his new stepmother intervened, and it wasn't often that she ran the risk of Michael's temper by doing that. Especially for a boy who had never shown the faintest inkling of affection or kindness towards her, despite how awkward a situation she'd now found herself in. She had thought that Michael and she were going to have a fresh start and raise their own family, but now she'd inherited hand-me-down kids who seemed to be nothing but trouble, no matter how hard Michael came down on them.

The beatings, the shaming, the piss-reeking child tramping off to school surrounded by a miasma of misery and embarrassment, none of it seemed to be enough. Michael just couldn't get the kid to stop doing it. This only served to make the boy's father more and more angry. He would not stand for this defiance. Especially not such a disgusting display of it. In his rage, he seized Gary by the piss-soaked legs and hung him out the window himself, dangling the boy beside the bedsheets, cursing and screaming at him all the while. From a distance, the neigbours likely had no clue what was going on with the sheets being slung out there every day to air, but the sight of a child being dangled by his ankles over a lethal drop was a different story. In his fury, Michael had ended up revealing his own secret shame much more clearly than he ever could have shown off Gary's little accidents.

Gary had been entirely convinced that his life was over when his father was holding him out the window. It wouldn't have even had to be deliberate. All it would take would be a slip of Michael's grasp and down he would have fallen again. Right onto his head. The last time had almost been the end of him. Some might even have argued that with the sudden change in his personality, the person that Gary was before his fall had in fact died, to be replaced by this sullen and miserable child. When he was hauled back into the room, for the first time since he'd had his accident, he was crying. All of his emotions had seemed muted after the fall, barring his rage, but this near-death experience seemed to have unlocked something new in him. Whether it was abject fear or some fresh, deeper well of misery wasn't clear.

That moment of madness didn't mark the end of this conflict, but it certainly seemed to temper Michael's behaviour for the immediate future as he became aware that he was being observed for signs of abusing his children by the neigbours. Neigbours who already didn't look kindly on a man who'd had a divorce then brought his offspring from that failed marriage back into his home, particularly since those kids were so ill-behaved they had to be constantly rebuked. With Michael's abusive behaviour somewhat mitigated, Gary wasn't living in constant fear, and his bedwetting became far less frequent. Consequently, the beatings became less frequent and the cycle of accidents and torment mercifully eased off.

At home, the rigid structure imposed by Michael benefitted Gary greatly, but at school, he still had the freedom to run wild with his natural impulsivity tempered only by his fear of the violence his father would inflict if he heard any bad report about him. For the most part, Gary's teachers got his best behaviour, even if he did seem to have trouble concentrating a lot of the time, but the other students treated him like a pariah. In truth, he more than earned it with his treatment of them and the outlandish things that he'd say and do for his own amusement. The real trouble with Gary was that he was self-aware enough to recognise that the situation wasn't working for him and he understood himself well enough to know that he needed structure and discipline to give the wild river of his thoughts and actions a direction. So, with that in mind, once he was a teenager he began campaigning for his father to transfer him to a military academy.

This would of course serve two purposes, it would give him the structure he needed to excel, and it would also allow him to finally escape from his father's iron grasp. His brother would have no easy way out of the house until he was 18, but Gary could see the light at the end of that tunnel rushing towards him.

Terry had never been the problem. He had never acted out, never defied his mother or father without the guidance of Gary, and both of his parents were thoroughly aware of that. As Gary set off to begin the remainder of his education at Staunton Military Academy, Ellen came back into the picture, asking for her boys to be returned to her, knowing that she would only get the one. Her life had stabilized in Gary's absence, she had remarried and was comfortable. The extremes of her emotional instability were curbed by the presence of someone else in the house to provide her life with some structure, but the one thing that continually made her depression flare-up was the memory of abandoning her children to the grips of the man who had made her so miserable. Gary had left and Michael was more than happy to be rid of Terry as well, though of course, he would never outwardly admit it. Instead, he used Ellen's latest crusade to reclaim the kids as a point of contention, the way that he always had. Regardless, the results were the same, Terry went home to his mother, Gary went off to military school, and everyone was happy with the results. Ellen was free of her guilt, Michael was free of the burden of raising his children, Terry was free of the terror that had ruled his young life for the entire time that he lived under his father's roof, and Gary was free of all of them.

One Boy's War

While Staunton Military Academy sometimes served as a dumping ground for ill-behaving children, and they had every expectation that Gary would be one of them, it was also one of the many institutions in the country designed specifically to condition the wayward youth of America into the perfect fighting force. It was a place where children who had never known discipline could learn it, but along with that they could acquire all the skills that would be required of them should they go on to military service, as was expected of all of them. Some resisted this process, they washed out and ended up back as civilians feeling as though they'd undergone some awful punishment, having all of their freedom taken away. Gary was not one of those who resisted. At fourteen years old, he knew he wanted to go on to a career in the military, a place where his often chaotic mind could be harnessed and driven towards a useful point. The fact that this decision had filled his father with pride in him for the first time in his life was irrelevant, he didn't do it because he wanted praise, and the idea of the old man respecting him, quite frankly, made him nauseous.

Within the walls of Staunton, he was not some bizarre outlier who was to be loathed for his differences, he was an excellent soldier who had already adapted to the new situation. If his instructors had realized that the level of unwarranted oppression that they inflicted on their students was several degrees lighter than he was accustomed to, no mention was ever made of it. He got along with the other students just fine, either because many of them were "bad kids" who were now being forced into a disciplined life for the first time, or because they too were devotees of the ultimate goal of joining the military.

For the first time in his entire life the intelligence that had always felt like such a burden to him, making him so different from everyone around him, was something to be praised instead of viewed with unease. There was constant and regular testing of the recruits as they proceeded through their academics and the more physical parts of their training. Benchmarks for them to pass that were clearly marked, goals that they sought to achieve, and each time Gary had to push himself to reach any one of these goals he felt a sense of achievement, again, for perhaps the first time in his life. This culminated in the IQ test.

The intelligence quotient test is greatly debated nowadays for its effectiveness, but at that point in history, it was considered to be one of the most important tools in the army's assessment arsenal. It allowed them to divide up those soldiers that scored under the global average of 100 into the non-skilled roles, and those that scored higher than the average into more specific roles within the military, based on their particular areas of expertise. Given the nature of Staunton, the majority of the students would score under 100 and could expect to spend their military careers progressing gradually up the ranks of the foot-soldier. Some that showed excellence or charisma might still end up funneled towards the officer programme, but for the most part, it was the moment of division between the haves and have-nots.

Gary scored 148 on his IQ test. It put him in the highest percentile of anyone attending the academy, including the teachers. Of all the people in the world, only 0.48% of them ever scored that high on an IQ test, and it put him among the ranks of top scientists and luminaries. The lower end of the range is where a person is considered to be a genius. This changed his prospects for the future considerably. While everyone else in the Academy would be funneled into one programme or another depending on how well they scored and what their aptitude was, he suddenly had the choice of any area of specialization that he desired. After graduating from the academy and going into military service, he would receive the training to become anything that he wanted to be. He just had to choose a specialist branch where he felt that he could best bring his excellence to bear.

The sense of superiority that he had felt throughout his entire life now seemed to be completely justified. Of course, he was better than everyone else – he was a genius. Even with everything that had happened to him, the damage that had been done to his brain, he could still outthink everyone around him. His behaviour went from completely ideal to manipulative. He no longer bore any burden without question or went along with what he was told without question; the things that had made him a good soldier, and the things that made him "special" ran in direct opposition to one another. It was difficult to obey orders when you knew you were smarter than the person giving them. It was difficult to dig a latrine alongside people with an IQ half of yours and feel like it wasn't a waste of your time. He developed something of an attitude problem, never directly contradicting his superiors, but always looking for an easy way out of any given situation. He began tricking and manipulating his fellow students into shouldering his burdens and completing his tasks with smug satisfaction as he circumvented the spirit of his orders and followed them to the letter. Where before he had been considered top of his class, his teachers now viewed his top grades with a degree of suspicion. Where before he had been accepted by his peers, he was now developing a reputation that he would never be able to shake off, as someone who'd rather talk than do. As someone who'd rather sit and think things through than follow his damn orders.

All that he had to do to get the career that he wanted in the military was to keep his head down and keep plodding onward through classes he was smart enough to teach and all the exercises that he felt were beneath him. Two years was not a long time to endure to achieve exactly what he wanted out of life, but somehow it was still too much for him. He dropped out just a short while before graduating to go back and live with his mother and Terry.

Neither one of them knew how to deal with him. The time away had changed him so thoroughly. The rampant tantrums that Ellen remembered were gone, but so too was all the softness. He'd left a boy and returned a man, scarred and strange to her eyes. Looking just enough like the husband she'd left that when he had an angry look in his eyes, she flinched in fear. Terry was delighted to see his brother again, but in their time apart, Gary's affection for the boy who he now considered to have been a burden through much of his life had waned. Absence should have made the heart grow fonder for the younger boy, but for Gary, who had done all he could to sever all ties with his family, never planning on seeing any of them ever again after joining the army, the experience was not a pleasant one. He lived with them, but he lived an entirely separate life. If they spoke to one another, it was out of necessity, not because Gary had sought it out, and those times when attempts were made to mend the bridges he'd burned, he would just shut down. He attended the same high school as his brother to finish out his education, but it was just as laughable as what he'd been learning in Staunton. He passed every test without study, knew every subject as though he'd written the textbook and while he enjoyed the attention that he drew from the girls in his class as a result of his newly built physique and the air of mystery surrounding him after his return, he formed no close friendships. The skills of manipulation that he'd begun developing at Staunton helped him to navigate the social situations he was placed in with aplomb. Fortunately, none of the awkwardness of his youth seemed to follow him but he had missed out on any opportunity for real human connection back then and now the purpose of making such connections seemed to elude him completely. He would date with the sole intent of having sex with the girls rather than to establish any real relationships. He would manipulate them into going as far as they dared but ultimately, they couldn't achieve the satisfaction of the steady relationship they craved, and he couldn't find the satisfaction that he was seeking with them, either. As for the boys in his class, he ignored entirely the ones that he couldn't force into obedience or trick into helping him. If they'd been a little more interesting, then it's possible he might have seen them as rivals, but he knew with unwavering confidence that he was better than all of them at everything that mattered, so it was difficult for him to feel much in the way of animosity. The feeling was not mutual, of course, but the dislike of the other boys was viewed by the girls as jealousy, which of course it was. And since the opinion of the girls he was trying to have sex with was the only opinion that mattered to Gary, he was quite content to let matters remain as they were.

His attendance was somewhat sporadic, in no small part due to the fact that his life was once again lacking in discipline and structure but also in a larger part due to the fact that he was mind-numbingly bored with the whole situation. Yet in spite of this, he had no trouble graduating at the head of his class, putting all of the previous academic all-stars to shame.

After school, he lingered for a while, still trying to seal the deal with the young women he'd been pursuing to little or no effect. He communicated with his mother and brother just barely enough information for them to grasp that he did not intend on staying in town for long. If it had been up to him, he would have left in the night without fanfare, but he was caught before he could depart with his suitcase containing barely anything at all. The sum of all his worldly possessions. A few changes of clothes and some manila envelopes of papers and basically nothing that distinguished him from anyone else. There were no tearful goodbyes, no heartbroken hugs, Gary had severed his ties with them long ago, and this was just the aftermath of that decision being played out.

He joined the army, as he had always intended to, even though his experience of what life in the army was going to be like had bored him so badly that he'd been forced to abandon it just months shy of graduation. Nevertheless, he remained convinced that the army would be the best place for him, and give him the best opportunities. In particular, he felt that he would make a far better officer than any of the people that he'd previously served under because he knew that he was much more intelligent than any of them, and therefore far more capable of making better decisions. He was also firmly convinced that he would be far more capable of emotionally manipulating those under his command into obeying his orders exactly. All of his records were transferred from Staunton Military Academy so his superior officers were immediately aware of his capabilities. On the other hand, the psychological evaluation that he had been quietly undergoing as part of that education was also passed along. This evaluation spoke of his particular behavioural quirks and suggested that he might be unsuited for certain roles within the army. He was rejected from the accelerated officer's programme almost as soon as he arrived, and his second choice, the military police, declined his application also. He had immediately sought out power over other people, rather than an area where his intellect could shine to its full potential, and where he, as a part of the army, could serve best. His rejections were relatively soft in comparison to most of the ones he'd faced in life, with a great emphasis on not wanting to curb his potential by putting him into a role that would not intellectually stimulate him.

It seemed that he actually took all of this under consideration and changed his career trajectory entirely, signing up for the medical programme. It was gratifying to see him choosing a role that would not play into the worst parts of his personality. Finding a position in the army that revolved around caring for other people ran almost entirely contrary to all of the assumptions that had been made about him, so he was accepted immediately and he began excelling with the same immediacy. The work was complex enough to keep him fully engaged without running the usual risk of boredom, and he was good enough at it that everyone involved in his training couldn't help but be impressed with him. He was qualified as a combat medic in record time, even finding enough additional time to take on some related electives before he was put into active duty.

In the aftermath of the Second World War, the American government had military bases all over the world, but some of the most important were in Germany. Following the fall of the Nazi regime, the overall rule of Germany had been split between the Eastern and Western blocs, with the USSR and the USA standing on opposite sides of the divide. If the Cold War were to ever turn hot, it was in Germany that most people would have expected the first blow to fall at that time. For that reason, the American military presence in the country was something of a contentious issue. Too many soldiers could be seen as a provocation, but too few might encourage belligerence. The balance was maintained very tentatively, with the best of the best from within the military structure being chosen to serve there. Given Gary's capabilities, it should come as no surprise, that was his deployment.

Working in the 46th Army Surgical Hospital on the Landstuhl base, Gary had a condensed career in medicine, studying and working his way to a full qualification that he could choose to use outside of the army as well. Most of the tasks he completed as a junior doctor were the sort of thing one might expect of a nurse, the practical tasks of treatment, but there was still enough intellectual stimulation in the "simple cases" that he dealt with to keep him engaged. The emotional detachment from his fellow soldiers actually did wonders for him when conducting those minor surgeries and procedures that were required of him. He did not flinch away from causing pain or drawing blood as other fresh doctors might. Instead, he performed his duties with an air of assured calm that often spread to the agitated patients, making life easier for everyone. He was just one of many doctors in the medical hospital so he was not able to receive the constant and steady flow of attention and praise that would have kept his ego sated, but he was doing so undeniably well in the role that it soon became apparent, even to him, that he could really make a go of a career in medicine. Here in the army, there may have been only a limited number of rungs in the ladder for him, but once he had completed his service and moved into private practice there would be money and the possibility of fame if he excelled as much as he fully expected to. He would likely never be a full-time surgeon with his now-rare lapses in awareness of the world around him, but there were still more branches of medicine in which he might excel. In Germany, away from the influence of his family, away from all the memories of home, away from everything that had made him into the person that he was, Gary was able to start anew. He was able to be a new, better person, setting aside the bad habits of his past and focusing on his work.

Then he got sick.

At first, it was just headaches, ongoing and regular. The headaches had been a constant companion throughout his life, ever since his accident. He had always brushed them off as irrelevant irritations that would fade on their own given enough time. Sometimes exacerbated by the concussions that he'd suffered at his father's hands, but never so bad that he couldn't function through the pain. Now the pain of them left him blinded and unfocused. He couldn't work, and he refused to go down the same route as so many of his coworkers, dosing themselves with the medicine meant for the patients, to keep on going past his limits. He began having to take time off when the headaches were at their worst. He was not even able to enjoy his time of relaxation because he had to isolate himself in darkness to keep the pain at bay. Next came the pains in his stomach, just as sharp and persistent as the headaches, but entirely new and unfamiliar. He'd put off seeking medical help for his headaches working off the assumption that they would eventually dissipate as they always had in the past. Typically, he had only suffered badly from them during times of stress, so he had hoped that as his day-to-day work in Germany became easier for him, so too would the pain fade. This new symptom had him convinced that this was something more than a simple stress reaction, however. After a bout of absences due to his illness, he contacted one of his superiors within the hospital to arrange an examination.

Due to the shift-based nature of work in the hospital, and the rate at which patients had to be attended to, none of Gary's superiors had spent any length of time in the same room as him. They knew of him primarily by his reputation as one of their most promising up and coming doctors but their interpersonal interactions had been limited almost entirely to issuing orders and moving on.

He had missed almost a full week of work before being seen, but the moment that he was in the room with one of the senior doctors, it was apparent that something was off. The pains in his stomach were easy enough to diagnose as symptoms of a bout of gastroenteritis that had been affecting many of the soldiers on base. There had been some bacterial contaminant in the local food supply that their immune systems simply weren't prepared for after spending their lives in America and it had caused widespread vomiting and diarrhea with one of the bunks having to be sectioned off and used as a quarantine area to prevent any further spread. What concerned the doctor were the other symptoms that Gary was showing. The headaches, in combination with his past head injury, could be indicative of something more serious, but likely wouldn't have been sufficient to raise alarm on their own. While they were talking about Gary's condition and how he had found travelling to Germany, about his taking up this new role and all the rest, the older doctor recognized a more concerning symptom. Something referred to in the medical field as "blunted affect."

Gary was not showing the full breadth of human emotion. In fact, he seemed to be mostly incapable of doing so. He was never happy, never sad, never anything at all, even when talking about things that should have provoked a serious emotional response. While there are many different medical conditions that can cause this, his doctor suspected that he was suffering from what was known at the time as schizoid personality disorder. This simply means that instead of suffering the full panel of symptoms typically associated with Schizophrenia, including all the usual hallucinations, he was only being affected by a partial selection of symptoms. Sometimes, particularly in young men, this was the prelude to schizophrenia fully manifesting. Clearly, that was something of a concern when the person who might suddenly start manifesting hallucinations and delusions was also the one holding a scalpel.

Of course, making such a diagnosis on the basis of a single brief conversation was out of the question – further study would have to be made to be sure of what they were dealing with. That was something of a problem given where they were. Giving Gary antibiotics to deal with his gastrointestinal issues, he was relieved of duty until he could be transferred back to America for further examination and treatment.

They had what very well could have been a ticking timebomb on their hands with Gary. Given his intelligence, clearance, and access, if he were to suddenly lose his mind, there was a considerable amount of damage that he could cause. The doctor had to take into account the safety of everyone on the base, not just his patient, so he also gave Gary a prescription for an anti-psychotic medicine called Stellazine, telling him that it should help to keep his headaches under control. The medicine was effective. The stomach pains soon faded, and so too did the headaches, yet at his follow-up appointment when he was fully expecting to be cleared to return to duty, he was not. The blunted affect remained in effect, and further questioning about his mental and emotional state left Gary more confused than anything else. Gary had the training to recognize these symptoms in others, but it had never occurred to him to turn the diagnostic criteria on himself, because to him, his mental state was perfectly normal. Even now, he was confused as to what the doctor thought was wrong with him, and why he was going to have to take the transatlantic flight back to America for further testing. But if there was one thing that he had learned over his years in the military and the academy preceding it, the best thing to do was to just follow orders and keep his head down until the matter was resolved. He didn't want to end up in the same position as he had back at Staunton, with a bad reputation and a desperate need to escape. Head down, do the work, stay calm and collected. He'd jump through whatever hoops the doctors wanted him to jump through then get back to doing what he was best at.

He was shipped back to Philadelphia where the veteran's hospital took over his care and a battery of further tests began to be applied to him. He was somewhat mystified by them but continued to answer as clearly as possible to try and get out of the situation and back to work. His blunted affect was noted again immediately, but the question soon became whether it was a result of schizoid personality Disorder, or one of a broader swathe of other issues that could be causing it, ranging from developmental disorders to some sort of gross damage to the brain tissues as a result of his childhood injury. He was poked and prodded, his blood was drawn and he was examined and cross-examined by a dozen different doctors, all trying to probe into why he was the way that he was. There was a family history of mental issues ranging from depression to behaviours that could be considered symptomatic of schizophrenia, and Gary himself had shown traits of emotional instability throughout his life history. The fact that the anti-psychotic medication that he probably wouldn't have been prescribed in a normal diagnostic procedure had cured him of his headaches seemed to suggest that there was some element of psychotic issues to be resolved, but once more this just raised more questions. His rapidly dwindling patience proved to be a helpful diagnostic tool too. It seemed that he was capable of expressing anger, if nothing else, which threw the initial symptom of blunted affect into question, except it was still extremely noticeable in every interaction with Gary outside of his mounting frustration.

Eventually, the consensus opinion was that there was no consensus opinion, each doctor seemed to have ended up with their own pet theory about Gary Heidnik, and few of them overlapped. They were all in agreement, however, that whatever was affecting Gary meant that he would be too much of a risk in his current position. The original diagnosis given to him in Germany was upheld, and he was taken from the military hospital to the army's base in Philadelphia, where he found himself in front of a panel of the highest-ranking officers he'd ever encountered. There he was informed that while his country thanked him for his service, it could not continue given his health conditions. He would be honorably discharged from service with a full pension immediately and barred from reenlisting for the rest of his life.

For the first time, the severity of the situation finally sank in for Gary. This was not some minor health concern that the doctors were making too much of a fuss over, this was about to ruin his life. He tried to plead his case for staying on in the army, but the decision had already been made. The future that he'd planned out was now snatched out of his hands. The order and structure of life in the army, gone. The guarantee of a slow ascent to greatness through the medical training he'd receive, gone. All the promise of his future had just been snatched away, and he knew as he walked out into the sunlight as a free man that he'd never get it back.

He didn't make it far, in his shell-shocked state, before one of the soldiers from the base came strolling up beside him. He might have been discharged, but the army still took care of their own. They got him set up with a motel for the night, pushed some cash into his hands so that he could enjoy himself a little now that he was free, and then they left him to his own devices.

There was nothing worse for Gary than being left to his own devices. He now had the freedom to go anywhere and do anything, and he was crushed once more by the awful burden of making decisions for himself. He had no work to occupy his mind. He had no dream that he was working towards. Everything that had given his life form and direction had vanished in an instant, and all that he'd gotten in return was an ongoing prescription for anti-psychotic medication.

He would not go home. He would not return to his parents, either one of them. They were the ones at fault, for the first injury to his head, or the many that followed, they'd caused whatever defect it was that the doctors had struggled so hard to find. They'd caused his dream to derail when it had just left the station after waiting so long. He was not going back. He wasn't going to suffer their contempt or their pity. Their sympathy would burn worse than any shame or torment that had ever been heaped on him.

Medicine was still within his reach. He had his training, he had a pension that he could use to support himself, and the GI Act following the war guaranteed him free education if he wanted to make something of himself. There was no need for him to go backwards. Fate had landed him in Philadelphia, and Philadelphia had a university where he could study medicine and become a doctor, he was still only 19 years old, and he would still be younger than the majority of the other students in the programme. His chance had not passed him by. And if he needed to make a little extra money in the meantime, there was no reason that he couldn't take on a nursing role at one of the myriad hospitals that filled the city. He filed his paperwork, proved his competence and became a licensed nurse practitioner at the same time he was making his application to the university.

One of these things went considerably better than the other, but neither of them went well. He struggled with the university work, not because he lacked the intelligence or interest, but because he fundamentally lacked the self-discipline that was required for a university format of education. In the army, he was bound tightly by order, but with the freedom to do as he pleased when he pleased, he soon found himself straying from what he should be doing, being drawn instead into hedonism. After only a single semester, his career at the university came to an end. His attendance was too poor for him to continue.

Meanwhile, his work at the Veterans Administration Hospital in Coatesville, just outside of town, was going about as well as his higher education. He was grossly overqualified for the work that he was doing, bored constantly and irritable the rest of the time. He had secured his job there thanks to his ties to the army, and their ongoing desire to take care of their own, but he soon proved to be an ungrateful recipient of such gifts. On multiple occasions, he was reprimanded for the incredibly offensive manner in which he treated his patients. What he'd considered to be a normal amount of brusqueness and jokes actually turned out to be ongoing abuse of the patients in his care, all of whom came to hate him quickly. The sociopathic tendencies that had helped him to be an excellent surgeon and doctor made him an awful nurse and an intolerable carer. Still, it is likely that if he had just been rude, the hospital would have kept Gary on in perpetuity. There was no shortage of sour-faced veterans left after the war, and the fact he was a little younger than most didn't change the fact that it was the army that had made him the man he was today, and they'd have to shoulder the burden of that. Of course, simply being obnoxiously rude to the people he was meant to be taking care of was not the entirety of Gary's faults. He was written up repeatedly for being late, unexplained absences and the endless moments where he abandoned his duties to go off and do as he pleased in the middle of the day. He didn't care about his job, he didn't care about these people, he didn't care about anything. His life had been taken away from him. His future was now so far beyond his reach that he didn't think he could see it anymore. He had gone from setting broken bones and readying himself to stitch bullet holes to changing bedpans and begging the clock to tick past the end of his shift.

They laid him off, and he could have kissed them for it. He hated the job, hated pretending like he cared about any of these useless, worthless people. It was a massive monument to failure, to soldiers too incompetent to avoid injury and the old and decrepit who would have been better off shuffling off the mortal coil while they still had some semblance of dignity left. But then again, he was one of them. One of the worthless incompetents that the army had let go because he was of no use to them in his current state. If he'd had any dignity, he would have walked right out of the honorable discharge, bought a gun and put it in his mouth, but knowing his luck, he'd just punch another hole in his ruined brain and end up drooling and pissing himself in the same hospital he'd just walked out of. Everything that he was, everything that he could have been, he'd lost it. All of his boundless potential reduced to this. All he was good for was nursing, and most of the hospitals in the city wouldn't touch him now that he'd been terminated. He'd had to call in favours to get that job, now what was going to happen to him?

He ended up back on what had to be the lowest rung of the ladder in the medical field. There were few hospitals set up to deal with the mentally ill in the 1950s but Gary found his way to one, and he was set to work immediately without his references ever being checked. Even if he'd been a stranger coming in off the streets with no more qualifications to be a nurse than a bricklayer, they would have taken him on because they were so understaffed it was brutal.

If he'd thought that the hours at the hospital were arduous, they were nothing compared to what he had to endure now. Twelve-hour shifts of "patients" medicated until they were little more than living corpses. The only benefit was that he could curse at them as much as he liked without anyone giving a damn. So long as they survived the shift, he'd done his job. Rotating the vegetables so they didn't get bedsores. Steering the mobile ones away from any sharp corners. It would have been tragic if he couldn't already see himself in their place. schizoid personality disorder was the beginning of worse things if they had managed to land on the right diagnosis. This was the sort of place that he could end up, being spat on by a washout nurse the same way he did to his own crop of morons.

There were few jobs in the world more miserable and thankless than caring for the mentally ill, and in the aftermath of the war, there were more mentally ill patients than had ever existed before. Psychiatry and pharmacology had finally joined hands to produce a new generation of treatment for those suffering the after-effects of the horrors that they'd witnessed. To Gary's way of thinking, this new generation of psychiatric treatment made the previous standard of care, one in which the mentally infirm were simply locked away out of sight, looked positively compassionate. At least the patients from that era were still themselves. Patients subjected to the newer treatment protocols could often end up locked inside their own body. Their medication rendered them incapable of acting; some were violently severed from parts of their own mind by surgery or electrocuted into submission in a vain search for a cure to their sickness. Those that got better were those who were always going to get better, those who were prepared to pull themselves out of their sickness to escape the circumstances that they'd sunk to. The ones that remained were the vulnerable, the weak, and those with conditions beyond the realm that modern medicine could yet touch. The kind that Gary lived in fear of becoming.

The job wore him down. The work was miserable. The living conditions for both patients and staff equally drab and dire. Before now, he could have managed to see his way through it because before there was always a light at the end of the tunnel, a way to escape from his current situation by pushing through to the other end of the suffering. Now he had no future to hope for. Now he had nothing.

Nothing except for a long family history of depression and easy access to pills that he was intimately familiar with. Pills that he could knock back one night after work, lay down to sleep, and never have to wake up and face another miserable day.

He made his first suicide attempt while still employed in the mental hospital, and when he realized his mistake in the dosage it was already too late. He went from being one of the staff to being one of the patients overnight, after they had discharged him from the infirmary where his stomach had been pumped. The patients were not closely monitored, but the medication was. It had value, after all. When his lethal dose had gone missing, it had been immediately reported, and the other nurses had gone to work rescuing and resuscitating him. There was no escaping this place. Even in death, he'd been dragged back. But where before he'd had some measure of control and power, now he was one of the victimised. He braced himself in those early days to be treated just like everyone else, to be tormented and loathed and looked down on, but it seemed that his attempt on his own life had been the catalyst for change in the facility. The other nursing staff had realized just how easily any one of them could have ended up on the other side of the pill line, and they had modified their attitudes. Gary actually received a decent standard of care from the people who used to be his co-workers and an unexpected degree of support and interest from the medical staff who were further up the hierarchy. Before he knew it, he was being discharged. For obvious reasons, he would not be allowed to resume his work there, nor could he pursue any further work in the medical profession where he might come into contact with the temptation to do away with himself in the same manner again.

Medicine had been his salvation. It was the one thing that whatever was wrong with his brain hadn't taken from him, and while he'd loathed working as a nurse practitioner, it was at least something that was his, something that he'd earned. He was struck from the registration now, with no hope of ever getting back in. Whatever he did in the future, it would not be in medicine. Whatever dreams he might have clung to involving getting his life together and going back to school to pursue the wealth and fame that he'd dreamed of were dead and lost as surely as if he hadn't been resuscitated.

In the years that followed, life did not get easier for Gary. He worked a variety of menial jobs, just trying to make ends meet but, on occasion, he found himself having to do the one thing that he never wanted or meant to do, he had to move back in with his mother for spells when he couldn't secure work for himself. There would be twelve more suicide attempts in those years. Some more serious than others, all of them ending up with him confined to a mental institution once more. Sometimes for extended periods of time and sometimes only for brief spells while he was monitored to make sure whatever method he'd used this time wouldn't have some unexpected, delayed effect.

By 1970, Gary's life was no different than it had been immediately after his first suicide attempt almost a decade before. He was fundamentally unhappy with everything in his life but couldn't find the impetus to do anything about it. The only difference between 19 and 27 was that he'd wasted eight years of his life doing nothing. All that boundless potential, all of the pressure that he'd put on himself to be something amazing had slowly but inexorably crushed him. He did nothing except exist, and he even tried to stop doing that on a fairly regular basis when the weight of the world grew to be too great a burden. He was a genius, a master manipulator, and with just a little help to get started, he could have been one of the most wealthy and powerful men in the world, but that first step towards a better life always eluded him. He just couldn't shake off the burden of missed opportunities. He was haunted by his own failure to the point that he couldn't even envision a world where he was a success.

That changed on Mother's Day 1970. While both his father and brother had made attempts on their own lives in the intervening years, Ellen had always managed to stay on top of her own mental health with the help of her new husband. Even with the intermittent stress of her washed-up son showing up with no advance notice to stay with them for extended periods, she had still found the stability that she needed to carry on. Her alcoholism had not diminished in the least, but as it had been throughout Gary's childhood, it remained at a level where she was at least functional. She would have described her drinking as "just taking the edge off" and that was essentially what it did, flattening out the spikes of her emotional instability into more of a curve. So long as she was never sober, she never had to deal with the worst of her illness. But eventually, everyone is confronted with a moment so sobering that they cannot ignore it, and for Ellen, that was a diagnosis of cancer. It had spread throughout her skeleton, cracking and weakening her bones, it was aggressive and in need of immediate treatment. Expensive and painful treatment and there was no guarantee the treatment would ultimately save her. She was looking down the barrel of a slow and ignominious death, where what little dignity she'd managed to cling to throughout her life would have been stripped away. It was a thought too hard to bear, a future too dark for her to want to endure any part of. In her kitchen, she gathered some cleaning supplies and her favourite mug, combined a lethal combination of mercuric chloride, and then walked down to the basement so that she'd be out of the way. Her body would not be found until the early morning hours after her husband, finally realizing that she hadn't simply gone out and failed to return at a reasonable time, had conducted a thorough search of the entire house. The police were called, along with an ambulance to cart the body away, but even if that ambulance had arrived immediately there was nothing that they could have done, given the particular lethal mixture she had made. In this, as in nothing else in her life, Ellen had been decisive and effective, leaving nothing to chance.

When Gary heard the news, he became nearly catatonic. His mother had been the only point of stability in his life for a long time, despite how unstable she was herself. She had been the one part of the past that his own troubled circumstances had forced him to cling to. He would attend her funeral still struck silent by the turn of events, but internally, his mind was racing.

It could have been him. It could so easily have been him if he'd ever properly applied his own incredible mind to the task of killing himself. He could have been the one being lowered into the ground in a pine box, having done nothing with his life. Having made nothing of himself. He could have died, living a life just as inconsequential as his mother's had been. Everything that he could have been, squandered.

He was not going to kill himself. He was not going to go on living this pathetic half-life either. She had been his last tie to the past, so now he let the past go. He could forget about her, about what had happened to him in his childhood, about the army, and the medical career that should have been his. He could set it all aside, now that he was confronted with the reality of his own mortality. It didn't matter how much time he had wasted, or how long it was going to take him to climb to where he wanted to be. He was done with being nobody. He was never going to have a smattering of gormless nobodies standing around his grave, faking grief. Ellen had not mattered. She had left no mark on the world, and she had done nothing for herself except going through the motions of what she thought a life was meant to be. Gary was destined for something greater. Some freak accident, long before his fall from a tree, had combined the genetics of two terrible, weak, people to create a mind so sharp that he could reshape the entire world, and he was damned if he was going to go on wasting that miracle.

RYAN GREEN

The House That God Built

He sat himself down with a pen and a sheet of paper when the funeral was done and he worked out what he wanted out of life. Power. Money. Family.

That last one may have come as something of a surprise, but in spite of loathing his own, Gary had a deep and abiding desire to have a family of his own, to raise children in his own image, a lasting bloodline legacy that would persist long after he himself had left the world. What he meant to build wasn't just a future for himself, but an empire that would stretch on throughout human history until the end of time. He wanted his name to be remembered forever. Legacy was the only way to ensure that.

He looked at his goals, looked at his skills, and looked at what he had available to him. Every asset that he could bring to bear amounted to a few hundred dollars in savings, the clothes in the wardrobe, and the little Bible that he'd taken with him from the church after the funeral ceremony was over. It was still tucked in the pocket of his black suit jacket, hanging on the back of his chair.

What was a job that a master manipulator could use to gain power and wealth? A job that required no arduous crawl through qualifications or up a career ladder. Something that he could start doing today that would get him everything that he wanted. He took the Bible out of his jacket pocket and stared at it. There had been no reason to take it, other than childish revenge for being forced to sit through the same repetitive sermons every Sunday. He didn't even need the book, he had it all memorized, more or less. That was what happened when you locked a genius child in a church with nothing to do but read or listen to the ministrations of the boring. He could have done that job in his sleep. Making little speeches. Bilking people out of their hard-earned money with the collections bowl. He paused on the idea.

Why shouldn't he? He may have had no belief in any power higher than his own, but the world was filled with gullible people who did, and if they ended up answering to him, wasn't that essentially fulfilling that very same contract? They would put their faith in an entity much more intelligent than them and ask it to make all their decisions for them, and he would reap the benefits of manipulating those decisions to his advantage. Who on earth was more like God than him? He had a godly mind, he was handsome and charming, who was to say that he wasn't some latter-day prophet?

Gathering his savings, he went down to the library to do some research into how one went about incorporating a church. It took a little time to find all of the appropriate forms and papers and longer still for him to gather the first few followers that he could list as his congregation. The bare minimum was five, so he set to work poaching them from local churches in the neighbourhood where he lived. His house became his church, and each Sunday, he would gather up everyone who could be gathered in his local area and preach to them. Many of the older generation resisted, in no small part because the locals were almost exclusively black, and he was as white as could be, but gradually he won over the more susceptible, and with their support, and donations, he was soon able to get the Church of the United Ministers of God recognized by the state in October of 1971. It was registered tax-free, as all religions were, and by the time he went to Merril Lynch Bank to open an account for the organization, money was already steadily flowing in.

He lived in a poor, black neighbourhood, and it was on his neigbours that he preyed as they prayed. Gradually it became clear to some of his attendees that Gary wasn't really interested in their spiritual welfare, and they filtered back out, but those left behind were true believers in his church, and in Gary as a prophet. He had a showman's glitz that attracted many to his house, but as smart as Gary may have thought he was, his ability to completely overwhelm the minds of others and make them subservient to him only seemed to work on a small specific subset of the community. The mentally disabled. Soon, those people who cared for the mentally disabled learned about his church and began bringing their wards in to participate in a place where they'd be made to feel welcome. Gary's rather milquetoast interpretations of the Bible seemed to have been dumbed down just enough to suit them perfectly, giving them some degree of religious education without running the risk of anything too complicated or confusing. His was a religion with all the sharp corners sanded off, a version of Christianity that emphasized the conservative values he held dear without ever getting into any contentious matters that might cause upset. All that he really had going for him was his charisma, but that seemed to be sufficient to hold his particularly unique audience enraptured.

During this time, he began several illicit affairs with members of his congregation, swearing them to secrecy, but giving them direct access to their God in exchange for the access they gave him to their bodies. Most of them lacked the understanding of what was happening to really explain it to their parents or guardians anyway, and even if any alarm was raised, nobody would believe that such an upstanding citizen at the heart of their community would ever do something so untoward. There was a racial aspect to this as well. A black preacher accused of inappropriate relations with a white girl in his congregation could have expected to be lynched, or at the very least lose everything immediately, while a white man plundering the innocence of a black community was entirely overlooked. There was little reported about "Bishop Gary" and the extracurricular activities he undertook with the women of the congregation, because of course, to these strongly conservative, but not particularly intelligent women, he was both the sole moral authority governing what they should do, and a victim of their seduction, rather than it being the other way around. None of them wanted to be known as the harlot that brought a holy man low, so none of them ever came forward and spoke up. Many of them were so developmentally challenged that even if they had realized they were being taken advantage of, it was entirely possible that they'd never be able to communicate it, or at least never communicate it with enough clarity that anything could ever be done about it. Looking at it from an outside perspective it seems obvious that Gary was abusing his position of authority, but for many of the girls, it was the first time that they were ever taken seriously as romantic or sexual partners, so it is entirely possible that they viewed it as a positive experience. For obvious reasons, no testimony was ever taken from them that could lead us to either conclusion about their perspective on events.

 The most important thing for Gary was that his coffers were now overflowing, not thanks to the paltry donations of his flock which scarcely amounted to enough to live off, but from what he did with that seed money. He took the money that he received and created an aggressive and risky stock portfolio that nonetheless paid off, and as a religious organization, any profit went directly into his pocket, bypassing government oversight entirely. With what he made from his investments, he began buying up property in the local neighbourhood that was in a bad state, gathering the faithful together to work on the homes under the guise of housing the homeless, until they were once again livable, and then making himself the landlord of those properties to ensure a steady income moving forwards. By diversifying his investments like this, he was able to ensure that if either the stocks or the properties started to falter as a passive income, he could still expect to see enough coming in to keep him comfortable. With both avenues of income working as intended, he soon began to amass a substantial fortune. With more money came more opportunities to make money, to improve the church that had been the foundation stone for what he was building. He began drawing in a larger crowd as the church became more prosperous, never quite big enough that they couldn't all squeeze into his home, but always on the brink of him having to rent out a hall or buy someplace to make a dedicated church. It made for a strange atmosphere, all of the church-goers crammed in, elbow to elbow in what should have been the man's dining room, standing so close to the preacher that most of them could reach out and touch him if they tried. It was an intimate kind of church, where every person felt like Bishop Gary was talking to them individually. Where any one of them could ask any question and expect a perfectly recited piece of scripture to suit their problem.

There was little that Gary really wanted to buy with his newfound wealth. He knew that he wanted to be rich, but there wasn't anything that he wanted to be rich for. He didn't eat any better than he had when he was in poverty, he didn't dress any better, and the only way that you might have guessed that he didn't fit into the impoverished neighbourhood that he stayed in were the cars that he kept parked outside. A white and silver Cadillac Coupe De Ville and a 1971 Rolls Royce. They were his only indulgence, the only way that he showed that he was one of the richest men in the whole area. Close to home, it paid better for him to appear humble, while when he went out cruising for prostitutes, he found that the flashy cars helped to win them over and convince them, without him having to flash any money, that he could actually pay them for the acts of obscenity that he meant for them to perform on him.

Gary began dating, rather than merely bedding, one of his congregants, Gail Lincow, in the mid-1970s. She was mentally disabled, as most of the attendees were, a black woman in her early 20s, and she was, to Gary's mind, the perfect starting place for him to create the next generation of Heidniks, to take over his empire when he was old. She was not capable of understanding how pregnancy worked precisely, and she certainly didn't grasp the ins and outs of contraception. She was entirely in Gary's power, with him making every decision in her life for the duration of their relationship. When she began to swell with the baby in her belly, she thought that she was getting fat. She was embarrassed about it and tried to diet. It was only when Gary sat her down and explained what was going on, with no small degree of repetition, that she came to understand that she was carrying his child. That she was going to be the mother of his child. If she had been a little more canny, it is possible that she might have been able to secure a marriage proposal from Gary, but he was not looking to commit himself to any woman unless he had to. He had learned from watching his parent's example just how badly a mismatched marriage could go, and there was no question, looking at his chosen bedmates, that they were not a good match. He was a genius, she needed help tying her shoes. Yet despite this, he had faith that the strange alchemy of heritage would provide his child with some measure of his gifts, just as he had somehow become what he was from the humble beginnings of his parents.

Over the months of her pregnancy, he began sleeping around again, mostly hiring prostitutes rather than getting involved with any women in the church this time around, but it wasn't exactly difficult to keep Gail in the dark about his activities. She was not a suspicious person by nature, and Gary was, of course, a man of God, so there was no possibility of him leading her astray. He would bring home and bed multiple women at the same time while she lay sleeping in the guest bedroom, all with her entirely unaware of anything going on.

She was back at home when she finally went into labour, with Gary having become so tired of her presence that he suggested she head back to spend some time with everyone before the baby arrived and they'd be together all the time, As such, she ended up going to the hospital to give birth. This proved to be something of a problem. While the actual childbirth went remarkably smoothly, all things considered, there was no father present, and the girl who had just given birth clearly didn't have the mental capacity to care for her new child. It was written up as yet another small tragedy in North Philadelphia and the baby was placed immediately into care. Gary Junior vanished into the system without a trace, and even if there had been one, who knew the legal trouble that Gary would face if he tried to retrieve the boy.

When Gail came home without the baby, Gary was enraged. He had put in all of that work, put up with that woman lingering around him for nine months, and at the end of it, he didn't even get to keep the baby? It wasn't right. It wasn't fair. That was his kid. What did it matter if the mother was too stupid to even breastfeed? He could have taught her what to do, just like he'd taught her everything else.

While it may have seemed that Gary did all of his work on a Sunday during "showtime" the truth was that the vast majority of his actual work took place during the week. He would do all the things that a normal church official would do, visiting the elderly and the sick, leading prayer circles and offering his time to those in need of compassion, but he also had a business and investment empire to keep him occupied. In particular, at about this time, he began to encounter the first problems that one might encounter as a landlord in a rougher area. One of his residents had decided to stop paying rent and use their money for drugs instead. Typically, the community would shame anyone who didn't pay Bishop Heidnik his rent, but there were always going to be certain fringe outliers who couldn't be cowed by public opinion. It was one of these that Gary went to visit in 1976.

It would have been a fairly routine confrontation for the resident of the house. He'd dealt with dozens of landlords trying to strong-arm him into paying before, but he knew the deal. He just had to sit tight until a court order came through and the cops came to drag him out. For so long as he stayed put, there wasn't going to be any moving him without that. Gary was not pleased with this response, to put it mildly. He informed the resident that he could either pay the rent, or he could leave the property and never come back. Again, it was the usual rhetoric landlords used to try to scare people into giving up their cash, but unlike every other landlord this guy had faced, Gary wasn't bluffing. He had no intention of getting the police involved in what he considered to be a private matter. If the man wouldn't leave, then Gary would make him leave. He attempted to force his way in past the door, only for the resident to hold his ground. He hadn't been expecting something like this, not on the first visit, and not from the landlord himself. They usually hired in muscle for this sort of shakedown. Sticking his head around the side of the door and keeping his shoulder braced against it, the resident mocked Gary, saying that he wasn't getting in. That it was his house now. That was when Gary pulled the pistol out of his pocket, rammed it into the gap between the door and the frame, and pulled the trigger.

It was luck, and only luck, that made that moment something other than a murder. At the sight of the gun, the resident had jerked his head back in fear, so the bullet only grazed across his cheek instead of going directly into his skull. At the sound of gunfire, the police were called, and while Gary managed to quite easily make his way inside the property he owned and rented out after that first shot was fired, it was Gary and not the non-paying resident that was dragged away in handcuffs. Apparently shooting at tenants who wouldn't pay their rent was illegal. Who knew?

One of the advantages of having a great deal of money was being able to hire a decent defense attorney instead of having to rely on the one that the state would have provided him. Gary managed to walk away with the charges dropped, after paying a small fine for having an unlicensed firearm. He spent one night in the cells of the local station, insisting that the whole thing was a mix-up, and the sad fact was that given a Bishop and a junkie on opposite sides of an argument, there was little question of who any jury was going to believe. The only mix-up was that Gary hadn't killed the man. If he had, he could have claimed self-defense and walked away without a mark, but he'd made the mistake of leaving his victim alive to bear witness against him. It wouldn't be a mistake that he'd repeat.

With that little unpleasantness out of the way and his property emptied of unwanted pests, Gary got back to focusing on the more important things in life. He had all the money he could ever spend. Almost total power over his congregation. Everything that he'd dreamed of after his mother's death belonged to him now. Everything except for the children he so desired. He had learned from his first mistake. When his next child was born, it would be in his home, and he would not let any agent of the government snatch it away from him. From amidst the sea of faces in his congregation, Gary picked out another young black woman by the name of Anjeanette Davidson. Anjeanette was very much like his first "girlfriend" in that she was mentally disabled to the point that the government would most certainly take the child away from her if she gave birth in a hospital. With his medical training, Gary felt confident that he'd be able to deliver the child without assistance, and if the mother happened to die in labour, he wasn't exactly going to be heartbroken over it.

While he was no more tolerant of Anjeanette than he had been of Gail, the moment that he got her pregnant he insisted on her moving into his house so that he could keep a closer watch over her. It put something of a damper on his usual swinging lifestyle, and the prostitutes of North Philadelphia certainly felt the loss of one of their biggest clients, but he endured, as he had so many times before, so that he could reach his goal. Anjeanette was quite smitten with Bishop Heidnik, and he maintained a more benevolent relationship with her for the most part. The typical rape and "corrective" violence that he had casually inflicted on Gail was absent this time around, and he hoped that it would all be worth it if the end result was his long-term goals being achieved.

If this was successful, it would be no difficulty for him to hire some help to take care of the baby, or simply crowd-source the task to members of his congregation. There were varying degrees of mental disability among them, and while his typical targets were in the lowest IQ range, that didn't mean he could not find uses for the more functional members of his church. He had no fear of the child being raised in an unhealthy or chaotic environment, because he himself had come from far worse than anything that he thought that they could muster and he had turned into the pinnacle of perfection, at least in his own eyes.

But when the time came for Anjeanette to give birth on March 16th, 1978, there were problems. Gary had never actually delivered a baby, nor did he have much experience with the ins and outs of the final moments of pregnancy in his private life. When Anjeanette began to complain of terrible pain, he had no way of knowing if it was the regular discomfort that he'd read about in his medical textbooks being amplified by her inability to understand what was happening to her, or if something was actually wrong that might cause harm to his baby. He persevered for as long as he could, trying to calm Anjeanette with all of his talents of manipulation, and trying to ascertain exactly what was happening with all his medical skills but ultimately he was deprived of any of the equipment that a hospital might have that would allow him to make an informed decision about the safety of the baby, and he had to concede defeat.

He loaded Anjeanette into his car and drove her to the nearest hospital, introducing himself to the staff not as the father of her baby, but as her priest. He was caring for those in his community by bringing her here, and he definitely had not impregnated a mentally disabled woman. Unfortunately, this distinction meant that he could not be in the room with her as she gave birth, the hospital policy reserved that space exclusively for family members. Anjeanette begged for Bishop Gary to be there, to hold her hand, to keep her safe, but they would not allow it. The labour was difficult and long, and the staff at the hospital were quietly surprised that her preacher lingered for the whole time and that none of her family had been called to her side, but they didn't know the complexity of her circumstances, and she was but one patient among hundreds.

Eventually, the baby was born alive and healthy as could be in spite of all the trouble it took to bring it into the world. A little baby girl that they let Anjeanette hold while they contacted child protective services to ensure that it was taken away from her as quickly as possible. The girl was named Maxine. Mother and daughter were moved onto the ward without Gary being informed, and Anjeanette lay there in bed, cradling the little life that she had brought into the world, dreaming about the future that they'd have together, the family that she would raise and all the normal things that a young conservative woman might have dreamed about. Marriage, grandchildren, family meals, all of the things that she had never known in her life, with the price of entry being nothing more than this beautiful little girl clinging to her chest. A nurse remained sitting at the bedside for the duration, to ensure the safety of the baby, as there was no guarantee that the mother – in her diminished mental capacity – wouldn't smother it or drop it. They were doing her a kindness by letting her hold the baby, at the cost of the baby's safety. It was a compromise that lasted only long enough for the relevant government agency to show up.

Gary slept in the waiting room while all of this unfolded, blissfully unaware that his dreams of a massive family were being snatched away from him. It was only when a nurse came and stirred him and brought him through to the ward to "comfort" Anjeanette that he discovered his baby was already gone. His opportunity had slipped through his fingers again.

He wanted a baby. He wanted dozens of them. He wanted a family to raise and mould in his own image. He had everything else. He deserved everything he wanted. He had taken himself from nothing to these lofty new heights, on the power of his incredible superiority alone, and the world was denying him the one last thing that would make him happy, and this would not stand.

There had been a mistake, he felt, with Gail. He had abandoned her when she failed him by letting the baby slip through her fingers, and while he felt no particular guilt about it because she was essentially a subhuman thing that he could use for sexual satisfaction and to incubate his children, that did not mean he felt no regrets. By showing just a little bit of kindness, and the lever of guilt over losing his child, he could have kept her around as a dedicated acolyte. He would not repeat the mistake with Anjeanette. There was still a use for her, and her devotion to him could be tempered through these trying times into something more solid and substantial than it had been before. He had her affection, her adoration and her worship, but now he had precisely the lever that he'd need to lean on to make her do anything he desired, regardless of how terrible. She would serve his purposes, follow his orders to the letter, and think nothing but the best of him all the way through. You couldn't buy that kind of loyalty with kindness or sweetness, only with shared trauma. Just as he'd bound his brother to him in their childhood, now he had a new disciple.

The mistake had been the hospital. He recognized that now. He was too soft with his girls, if they died, then they died. If the babies died, then the babies died. He had been too focused on the single prize to think about the grand game. What he needed was to maintain control over the situation, regardless of how they might have felt, or how they might have feared. Everything needed to be kept in-house from here on out.

Anjeanette would remain his breeding sow, to be used once her body had recovered enough to be functional and capable of carrying his mighty seed once more, but sequential pregnancies with all the associated risks were liable to cause ever-increasing danger to the mother and children. He needed to spread out the risk, the way that he did with his investments. That meant that when one of his investments failed, the others could still pay off. He'd been putting all his eggs in one basket with this plan, and he knew that it was bad planning. He just had to step up and integrate his usual level of thinking into the procurement of his children. It was time to start handling this professionally.

Down in the Dark Place

Anjeanette had a sister. Her name was Alberta, she was a few years younger than Anjeanette, and she had been placed in the care of an institution for the developmentally disabled in Penn Township by their parents several years before Gary and Anjeanette had ever crossed paths. While Anjeanette was barely functional in society, Alberta had somehow been even worse off, with an intelligence comparable to a preteen child. She was utterly incapable of caring for herself, utterly incapable of clear communication, essentially incapable of anything that would be required of a human being living out in the world. The institution where she was housed had seemed like a cruelty to her, like she had been abandoned by her family into the hands of strangers, but in the 1970s it was one of the kinder options that were available. She had always been a background detail in Anjeanette's story. Something that Gary had filed away for later without giving much serious consideration. But now that he had his newly assembled plan for the future, she became a key component.

    He looked into the Harrisburg State Hospital where she was kept, studied the information that was available about it, and made a decision. It was not a place where he felt that anyone would notice Alberta's absence. The kind of mass incarceration that he himself had suffered through many times in his suicidal years. Freeing her was going to be a simple enough matter, thanks to their policies. He himself couldn't just wander in, pick out the prettiest mentally disabled girl and stroll out with her, but if he had a family member along, then he was free to take whoever he wanted. Anjeanette became the key to taking Alberta. It was a good thing that he had kept her sweet all along. Sweet and stupid, the perfect combination. She would go along with whatever he said, not only willingly, but with delight, and so long as Alberta was out of her direct line of sight, she would almost immediately forget about her. He made preparations at home before they set out to collect the girl. Clearing space in his basement, putting a bucket and some blankets down on the floor in the storage cupboard that he had down there, and fitting a lock to the outside. He knew exactly what he intended to do in the coming days, and if it was as successful as he suspected it would be, he would roll out the operation on a larger scale. Alberta was the test case, to prove that his plan was going to work.

They arrived at the Harrisburg Hospital together in Gary's car, but he encountered a minor roadblock almost immediately. Anjeanette didn't want to go inside. She was afraid that if she ever went into one of these institutions, she would never be allowed to leave. Not an unfounded fear, given it was essentially what had happened to her sister, who had gone in to give her parents a respite from their caregiving duties but was never collected and brought back home again. Typically, Gary could browbeat her into saying and doing anything that he wanted at any given moment, but the net result was often messy. She would burst into tears, snot would smear her face, he'd have to spend more time building her back up to a basic level of humanity than it had taken to break down her resistance, and today he couldn't deal with all that. Not if he wanted to make sure that the impression he was making on the Harrisburg staff was good enough for him to pull off this minor heist.

It probably made things easier for him, acting like the beleaguered carer for the girl's sister, playing up her incompetence and the kindness that he was doing in taking on the care of yet another one of them so that they could spend the day together and go for a little outing. It probably didn't hurt his case that taking one of their patients off their hands for a while would surely take some of the pressure off the already overwhelmed staff at the facility as well.

There was some initial reluctance to turn Alberta over to this man who was essentially a stranger to her, but her sister's presence was noted, and according to the regulations that governed who could and could not sign out residents, family members were included. Because Anjeanette was there, they really didn't have any grounds to deny the request for a day pass, and Gary was nothing if not persuasive. He was the family's preacher taking two special needs girls from his congregation for an outing, it was hardly going to end in trouble. They let him in to visit Alberta while they hashed out the details of the arrangement among themselves, as much as a test of his character as to see how she would respond to this stranger. He had her eating out of the palm of his hand within moments of sitting down. She had never been the most cooperative patient, so the fact that he could win her over so effortlessly really impressed on them that he would have no trouble managing her throughout her little excursion. The paperwork was signed off, Alberta got her day pass, and she walked out to greet her sister with a big smile on her face.

The two of them hugged in the parking lot, and the staff, still looking out, might just have felt a little pang in their hearts at the sight of it. It didn't take much convincing to have Anjeanette climb into the back while Alberta got the big treat of sitting up front, and if she noticed that her boyfriend's hand, which usually fell to rest on her thigh in a possessive grip when he wasn't changing gears, fell onto her sister's instead, she didn't put things together enough to understand that there was any sort of problem. As for Alberta, who had never received anything resembling sex education, or the correct amount of physical contact, she was simply delighted to get a bit of attention.

The delight continued throughout the day, as Gary took her on the long drive back to his house, and they had a delicious meal bought from one of the local fast-food restaurants. The kind of greasy treats that she was never ever allowed to have on the strict diet that the Harrisburg Hospital kept her on. The excitement and enjoyment were tempered by the knowledge that at the end of the day, she was going to have to go back to her little cell in Harrisburg, but after dinner, Gary made an announcement. He'd spoken to the people in the hospital, and they'd said it was completely okay for her to spend the night here, having a sleepover with her sister.

He had made no such arrangements, obviously, they were entirely outside the purview of the day pass that he'd secured, but what the girls didn't know couldn't hurt them.

Both of the girls got changed into pyjamas, but at the last moment, Anjeanette noticed the problem with the arrangement, there was no bed for her sister to stay in. She certainly couldn't share the bed that Gary and she slept in, that wouldn't be proper. Gary reassured both girls that it was alright, he'd set up a place for Alberta in the storeroom in the basement. When it was time for them to go to sleep, he'd take her down and tuck her in.

They all stayed up way past their usual bedtime, until both of the girls were drooping on the sofa, then Gary took Anjeanette to bed and made sure she was settled before turning his attention to her sister. She should have felt some apprehension as she was brought down the stairs into the dimly lit basement, but she didn't have the wherewithal to understand that the situation was unusual because she'd been cloistered away for so long.

When she saw what passed for a bed, little more than a heap of rags, she might have made some complaint or might have just accepted it as a temporary solution, since she was so bone tired already after all the excitement of the day. Gary closed the door behind them and waited in her room until she had clambered into the makeshift bed, then he tucked her in, just like her parents used to do. He asked her if she wanted a goodnight kiss, and she was so dozy and happy that she said yes without thinking. It was not like the little pecks that her parents or her sister had given her over the years. His lips moved against hers and then she was scandalized to find his tongue slipping inside her mouth. She gagged and jerked back, but Gary already had the right words ready to soothe her. She had never been kissed like that before, because before, she was a little girl. She was a big girl now, all grown up, and that was how grown-ups kissed. Still unsure, but absolutely thriving from all the attention, she let him kiss her once again. When she felt his hands roaming over her body, she didn't stop him, because she was so afraid of letting him know how little she understood about life. She didn't want him to think she was just some silly little girl who couldn't do grown-up things. When he climbed on top of her and pushed himself inside of her, it burned and it hurt and she bled, but she stifled her cries and just sobbed softly to the side as he took his pleasure from her.

When it was over, he sat there by her bed, stroking her hair and telling her what a good girl she'd been. How she was going to be able to stay here with him and her sister for as long as she wanted to, so long as she went on being a good girl, but if she was bad, he was going to send her back to the bad place where they said that she belonged. She wanted to be good, and live out here in the world, didn't she?

She was traumatized and confused, but also desperate to prove that despite that, she was a good enough girl that she could live outside like her sister. If this pain was the price that she had to pay to get that freedom, that evidence that she was equal, then she was willing to endure it.

Not that she had much of a choice. After their conversation was over, Gary showed her the bucket, in case she needed the bathroom through the night, and he locked her inside, turning off the single swinging bulb that illuminated the room as he went.

The next day, everything had gone back to the way that it was before. Anjeanette and her sister got to spend the whole day together, eating snacks and watching television while Gary did his work, then as the evening rolled in, he went out and got them yet another delicious meal to share, along with a bottle of wine that made both of the girls feel really grown up, and more than a little bit woozy. Their grasp on reality was tentative at best even on a good day, so with the application of alcohol things got even more hazy. Gary was sitting on the sofa in between them as the TV made loud noise and bright colours, and his hand was on Anjeanette's thigh, the way that it always was. And when he leaned in to kiss her, she didn't even remember her sister was there, let alone that she might be mortified by what was happening. She fell back into her seat, breathless after the kiss, and didn't even notice that Gary had turned the other way, to kiss her sister in exactly the same way.

He went back and forth between them, building up to the moment that they'd realize that the other was there and he could take things to the next level, but Anjeanette was too drunk to grasp what was going on, even when he suggested that maybe her sister could share the bed with them that night. She couldn't grasp what he was actually suggesting, so she told him that it wouldn't be big enough for all three of them. He misunderstood, taking it as a rejection of the idea of a threesome. Things were not stable enough in the household for him to force the issue, not with Alberta's emotional state to manage on top of Anjeanette's. He could handle manipulating one of them at a time but didn't want to push his luck and risk the two of them uniting against him and standing up for one another. He backed down, helped Anjeanette to her bed, settled her into her drunken stupor, and then took Alberta down to the basement once more.

That night, the pretence fell away. He trusted in the thickness of the walls to muffle any sound, and in Alberta's drunkenness to cover for any missteps he made. The night before had been a seduction as much as a rape, tonight there was no attempt made to get the mentally disabled girl with the intellectual capacity of a preteen in the mood. Pinning her down on the mound of rags he'd given her as a bed, he raped her repeatedly throughout the night until even his apparently endless appetites were sated, then without another word, he left her locked in the dark, aching and sobbing with confusion.

It was early afternoon by the time Anjeanette woke up the next day, and she moved through the house in a daze until she found Gary working away as usual, and when she asked after her sister, he told her that she'd gone back home in the morning. She'd been too lazy to get out of bed, so she'd missed her opportunity to say goodbye.

In the weeks that followed, Anjeanette never asked any more questions about her sister. Never pushed to go and visit her again. She had hazy memories of the night before her sister's departure that she could keep set aside and pretend were just bad dreams, but seeing Alberta was sure to confirm her worst suspicions, and she didn't want her little paradise to crumble around her, so she kept her mouth shut. Besides, she hadn't liked all the attention that Alberta was getting from her boyfriend. He hadn't tried to have sex with Anjeanette once while her sister was there, and that was usually something that happened every single night that she stayed over.

In the days and weeks that followed, his interest in her seemed to wane even further. He had always pressured her to do things that she wasn't comfortable with. Things that she was convinced were naughty in a way that God wouldn't be happy about. Sometimes she'd indulge his grotesque desires but now she was sore down there, and already in a bad mood about his perceived rejection of her. He would never ask, just tell her what he planned to do, and see how much of a fuss she kicked up. Then there would be the usual recriminations, the crying, the manipulation that she never quite seemed to recognise, and finally the compromise, where she'd do what he asked, or at least some portion of whatever filthy, degrading thing he wanted to do to her. But now, when he told her what he meant to do, she said no, and that was the end of the conversation. He'd just up and leave the bed and the room without a second thought. The only times he did stay were when she gave no hint of resistance, when she acceded to his demands, no matter how vile or painful they might have been. And she did give in, just to have his attention, just to feel like she was still secure in the relationship, but for some reason that didn't seem to make Gary any happier. He'd get to do whatever nasty thing he wanted, but he still didn't seem satisfied.

On the nights when she rejected him, he'd leave their room, go downstairs to the basement for a few hours, and come back seeming happier than ever. Whatever he was doing alone seemed to calm him down a lot more than her willing submission ever could. Throughout the days that followed Alberta's departure, Anjeanette didn't notice anything out of place, or out of order, other than the fact that the man she treated as her husband had lost sexual interest in her. She didn't notice him carrying food down to the basement. She didn't hear any unusual sounds coming from the basement. She didn't know that there was anything going on whatsoever. Whether this is due to her mental disability or due to the degree of care that Gary took to obscure reality from her is unclear, but there is a distinct possibility that it was exclusively the former. Gary didn't really seem to care what she thought or knew. He believed that he had complete domination of her and that no matter what she learned of him, she would come crawling back to heel regardless. He lived in a world without the possibility of consequences. King of his own domain. Where he could bully, outwit, and talk his way out of anything.

Alberta's absence had not gone unnoticed. The police were not informed immediately, as there had been cases in the past where a "day pass" was misinterpreted to mean 24 hours outside of the facility, but almost immediately after that, the police were informed of the girl's abduction, and her circumstances. The police took the name of the person who had signed the girl out and then sat on it for several days before running it through their records and identifying Gary Heidnik as their most likely perpetrator. His history with the family was known, he had a criminal record, albeit one that had little correlation to the current situation, and he had been bold enough to sign his own real name into the paperwork at the hospital. Even so, the police decided to tread carefully. They knew that the man was some sort of religious leader, and they'd dealt with faith healers and their like throughout recent history, creating a massive stink when those that they were "healing" or had "healed" were taken back into custody.

They arrived at his house with staff from the hospital to retrieve the girl, and with little more than a sigh, Gary took a step back from the door and invited them in. They followed him down into the basement and were almost immediately overcome by the open-sewer stench emanating from the locked storage room. He released Alberta, and she came scurrying out into the light of the basement, flinging herself into the familiar arms of one of the white-clad hospital staffers that she'd hated so much before. Prior to this, she had been communicative to the point of being a nuisance, but her experience in the basement of Gary's house seemed to have robbed her of her ability to speak entirely. She shook violently the entire time, and she was escorted up and out into the daylight as quickly as the staff could move her. Gary didn't bother with much in the way of excuses, just said that the girl had been enjoying her time here with him and her sister and didn't want it to end. The fact that she was a traumatized wreck didn't dissuade him from that story, or even fully convince the police that what he was saying wasn't the absolute truth. They knew the girl was mentally disabled but had no idea how bad she'd been before this little sojourn, so they viewed the whole situation as having been handled.

She was driven back to the hospital, and the police went their own separate way, considering it to have been a waste of their time to show up at all. That was until they received a follow-up phone call from Harrisburg. On her return to the hospital, she underwent a series of examinations and medical tests. These had determined that she had been raped both vaginally and anally and had contracted gonorrhea as a result. She was not capable of consent even if she had not been subjected to brutal force as indicated by the obvious signs of physical and psychological trauma. Her parents would have to be informed, and Gary Heidnik needed to be taken into custody for her kidnapping and rape before they could make that call, otherwise, there was a distinct possibility that there would be a murder in the very near future.

Gary turned himself over into their custody without complaint, explaining to the cops even as they were arresting him that this was all just some misunderstanding, and he was sure his many expensive lawyers would get everything straightened out in no time at all. Whatever lies Gary might have told about other things in his life, his statements regarding the quality of legal assistance that he had bought were never once proven incorrect.

They pounced on every one of the charges like terriers with a rat, questioning, prying, demanding evidence, and above all demanding that their client be allowed to face his accuser in court as the law so explicitly stated was required. Before the trial even got in front of a judge, they hammered on that last point, and the fact that there was absolutely no evidence that he was the one who had perpetuated the acts of sexual violence on the mentally disabled girl. Not even a statement from her making that accusation. This was all just supposition and circumstantial evidence. Everyone involved knew that Gary was guilty. From the parents of the two girls, he'd essentially been raping, to all the hospital staff who'd failed to safeguard her, to every single one of the police who'd touched the case. Everyone knew that he had done exactly what he was being accused of, but they couldn't prove it. Not with the surety that they needed to guarantee that if he was sat down in front of a jury he would be charged.

Alberta had never accused him. Alberta had never even talked about what had happened during her time outside the hospital. No matter how the staff or psychologists questioned her, nobody could get her to talk again after the horrific trauma that she'd been through. She had gone from one of the kindest and friendliest of the patients to one of the most withdrawn. There were patients on the deep end of the autism spectrum who were now more capable of communication than she'd become.

Without her statement, the case was weaker than it really needed to be, but still strong enough to ruin Gary Heidnik's life. He had his day in court, charged with a whole list of crimes: kidnapping, unlawful restraint, false imprisonment, interfering with the custody of a committed person – and most gruesomely – both rape and involuntary deviant sexual intercourse. The final charge on that list was a separate, more punishable offence in 1970s Pennsylvania and was usually reserved as an additional deterrent for cases involving homosexuality but correctly applied in this case due to the litany of sexual activities that he forced the poor girl to endure. She could not speak at his trial, any more than she had been able to in the months leading up to it. Even without her, the prosecution was able to secure a win, and Gary was sent to Graterford prison to serve hard labour.

It was a brief stay. His lawyers immediately brought his case up on appeal to the higher courts, and within only a few months they had his original sentence overturned. A great deal of information had been withheld by the court, with the prosecution having implied more than they could actually say regarding the events that had taken place between Alberta's abduction and retrieval. In addition, the court had never been allowed to take into account that Gary Heidnik was so profoundly mentally ill that he'd received an honorable discharge from the military as a result, as well as a prescription for potent anti-psychotic medication which he had not been taking for many years. All of the things that Gary had kept hidden from the public during his rise to power and wealth had suddenly switched from being a terrible burden of secrets to being his salvation. Taking everything into account, from the weakness of the original prosecution case to Gary's medical condition, it was extremely easy to argue that there was a different way that events may have played out, completely different from the way that the police had presented matters, one in which two people with diminished capacity collided and misunderstood one another. There was obviously no way that Gary could be released back into society if he was capable of such actions as a result of misunderstandings, but that did not mean that he should be punished to the full extent of the law as though he had deliberately abducted and viciously raped a girl.

He *had,* of course, but that was not the picture that Gary's very well-paid lawyers painted, and with that new possibility overlaying all of the facts of the case, it seemed to fit. His conviction was not overturned in the higher court, but his sentencing was. Instead of serving out the decade or more that would have been justice, he was instead transferred out of prison into a mental healthcare institution where he would receive treatment for his condition and move back towards being functional. Money was the measure of a man's success, and for him to have been so successful, he must have been a useful, contributing member of society who was worth rehabilitating.

It probably helped that Gary, who had always been something of an oddball, was becoming increasingly strange since being locked up in jail. At his first parole hearing when it was decided that he would be moved to a mental health institution, he went through the entire process without saying a single word, allowing his advocate to do all of the talking for him while he just sat there. When asked why he wouldn't speak up in his own defense, he gestured to his throat and shook his head to convey that he was incapable of speech. When pressed for a reason, and handed some paper to write on, he explained that he could not speak because "the devil had put a cookie in his throat."

Whether this was an example of his usual eccentricity pushed to the limits by stress or a part of a calculated move to make himself appear insane so that his legal team had more ammunition was entirely unclear. Even to his legal team. The end result was the same, however. His erratic behaviour was now being observed, rather than simply being a silly story that his friends would share. He was judged to be insane under the legal definition and was moved out of prison.

After a year in the first institution, he was moved to another. Then again the following year. He spent his third and final year in yet another mental facility where little to nothing had changed. He had been medicated for the duration of his tenure in the institutions and was a little more sluggish as a result, but otherwise, he had remained essentially identical to the way he presented himself on the first day that he arrived. Therapy seemed to have no impact on him whatsoever, but neither could any amount of assessments ever come to the conclusion that he was actually unsafe to be around people. When taking his medication, he seemed to be entirely in control of his emotions and behaviour, so by the time he'd departed the first institution it had already been more or less decided that he was safe to go back out into the world in spite of the horrific crime that he had committed. It was just a matter of passing the ball around until everyone felt like he had been out of sight for long enough that it would be acceptable to release him.

What Is Owed

In April of 1983, enough time had apparently passed. He was released into the supervision of the state's mental health programme and returned to his normal life.

Except his normal life was notable in its absence. Anjeanette had been taken back by her parents. His home where he had built his church was gone. There was no way that he could go back there and expect things to go on as they had, not with every single member of the congregation so painfully aware of what had allegedly gone on just beneath their feet. Of course, he had been greatly overestimating just how much the congregation actually knew about his crimes. Anjeanette and Alberta's family certainly hadn't been spreading the news. They were a small conservative family of limited means, and they had no intention of butting heads with the religious leader in their community. They just took their daughter out of the situation and moved to a new church.

Alone again, Gary set about rebuilding. The United Church of the Ministers of God had fallen into disrepair in his absence, with most of its success being built on the back of his charisma and acumen. His investments had been sitting idle without instruction on what to buy and sell. He sold off his old house and moved into a trailer, sleeping on the streets of southwest Philadelphia while he made plans to purchase a new one. He was out there among the homeless and the destitute, with a Rolls Royce and Cadillac parked in garages in the better part of town where they weren't liable to be stolen and the equivalent of half a million dollars in his accounts.

Eventually, he selected a new property. 3520 North Marshall Street, in North Philadelphia, just beside Fairhill and Kensington, closer to the city centre than he'd lived before, and slightly more upmarket without being too nice an area for his congregation to feel comfortable. The people who supported him and funneled their money into his church, believing in his message, were not wealthy people. They were the downtrodden and destitute. The working class and the underclass. People who had no hope for their worldly future, so pinned it all on the spiritual one. People for whom giving themselves over entirely to the will of a higher power was their only hope. How unfortunate that the higher power that they'd chosen to put their faith in was Bishop Gary.

He made a tentative approach back towards his original followers once the new place was purchased, once he knew that he was going to need a lot of free labour to get it up to his standards. If he had lost his congregants then and there, it is entirely possible that he might have simply abandoned preaching entirely. It wasn't as if he needed them anymore, at least financially. He made far more from his investments than he ever could from the collections dish, but they fulfilled a deeper need in him. The need to be worshipped. The need to be the centre of attention. The need to feel like he was important, not only to himself but to the whole world. If news of what he had done had spread, if his self-deluding followers had believed it and allowed doubt into their hearts, then he would have lost that, along with his most ready supply of victims to prey upon. But if even a few of them still remained, who had remained true and faithful even after hearing the most terrible things about him, then he knew then and there that they would follow him into the mouth of hell itself. If they had given themselves over to him that much, then they had put too much of their own self-worth on the line to ever back down and believe anything bad about him, because of what it would then say about them.

News had not spread. The family of his now ex-girlfriend had departed in mortified shame without saying a word. There would be no great test of faith, but neither would there be any battle to fight. He was going to be able to slot right back into the community that he had so brutally betrayed without any of them being even slightly aware of what had occurred.

With the church being re-established, the money and attention began to flow once more, but Gary was not satisfied. He should have been. Everything that he thought that he wanted, he was getting, but after his experience with Alberta, it all felt hollow. He'd tasted real power, the power of absolute control over another person, and now he didn't want to give it up. When he had been arrested, he had lost more than just his freedom, he had lost his wife.

He'd never married Anjeanette, and never would have, given how much he looked down on her, but she had still fulfilled the same role in his life as a wife would have. Now that she was gone, he found himself not only missing her more than he could have anticipated but angry about that fact. Society had taken his wife from him, and he had no means of taking her back. If he involved himself any further with that family, if he fought with the parents of the girl he'd kidnapped and raped, there was no question that the truth of the matter would come out. He wanted a wife, he was due a wife, they had taken that from him. But where others might have found themselves desolate at their loss or stopped in their tracks by the sudden derailing of their life, the same cannot be said for Gary Heidnik, who throughout all of his self-inflicted trials and tribulations remained active, if nothing else. Where others would have been stopped by such a turn of fate, the same cannot be said for him. He instead immediately began laying out plans to counter his loss. For all that he might have played at chaotic madness when trying to pass for insane, there was a clockwork quality to his mind, always ticking over, always pressing him forward.

So, with the same directness and logic with which he'd won himself a congregation and a fortune, Gary sought out a wife. He considered his first attempt to produce an heir to his empire an abject failure and put it down to the problems of modern society. Women's liberation movements abounded throughout the 70s, and by the time that Gary began this new search for a wife, he found that almost every woman that he encountered had a thoroughly modern view of things. They did not wish to be property, chattel, or breeding stock. They didn't want to be housewives or mothers. They wanted to be recognized as full people, and that was something that he could not tolerate. He lacked the means to step back through time to when women were subservient to their husbands in the USA, but there were still places in the world where he believed that women were still raised to know their correct place in the order of things. Through a matrimonial matchmaking service, he was put into contact with a young woman in the Philippines named Betty Disto.

According to her writings, Betty was absolutely perfect for him. Religious, dutiful, and interested in fulfilling exactly the role that he had cast for her in his mind, the obedient wife. The full material of their correspondence has been lost, so exactly how honest either one of them was with the other will never be entirely clear, but it seems at least somewhat likely that both Gary and Betty were upfront about their desires for the future of their match. Both intent on marriage, children, and raising a large family.

After two years of correspondence, the pair would finally meet in September of 1985 when he paid for her to fly in from the Philippines and picked her up from the airport. From there on, it was only a month or so before they tied the knot during a trip to Maryland. Judging by what is known of Gary Heidnik, it seems unlikely that he won her over with any great acts of romance, but it seemed that he must have at least partially fulfilled her expectations of what a husband should be. Or at the very least still seemed like a better option than returning to her homeland. There wasn't much of a honeymoon, as the two returned to his home in Philadelphia within a week of their wedding ceremony. Gary simply had too much going on to abandon his work for any extended period of time, and he didn't see much point in having a wife if she wasn't doing what he'd bought her for.

In spite of his sky-high expectations, at the beginning of the relationship, it seemed as though Betty was going to fulfill them. The house, which had previously been in a state of disarray and disrepair ever since Gary had moved in, was slowly transformed into something that resembled a family home. He had an outlet for all of his sexual energy that didn't require prostitutes or tricking people into subservience. Overall, it seemed as though this should have been the turning point in Gary's life when he started to get it all together. He had the wife, the career, the respect of the community, but it wasn't enough. Something was still missing, something that he'd felt before but that now seemed to be slipping through his fingers as he became a "normal" man.

As a consequence of this unsettling feeling, he began looking in all the wrong places, trying to find that elusive thing that was missing.

At first, he simply intensified the situation at home; he demanded perfection at all times, demanded sex at the drop of a hat, demanded something incessantly, trying to push his new wife to a breaking point, to prove that she was just the same as American women when it came down to it. This test failed, or rather, Betty passed. She couldn't be goaded into refusing him anything, even when he started pushing the limits of what she found acceptable in their intimate time together. She wouldn't say no to him, so he never had to apply any force or trickery to get his way. That was why these victories felt hollow. That was why he wasn't getting the same satisfaction as he used to.

With that failure, he remained oblivious to his actual desires, thinking that it was simply the monotony of sex with the same woman that was causing him to become bored and despondent. Even though the couple had barely been together for a few months, he started finding other women. Women in his thrall from the church, women that he paid for their services, and even women that he just picked up off the street using his natural charms. At first, he would take them to hotels, staying out all night, only to return in the dawn hours to find his dutiful wife waiting for him with his breakfast already on the table. He found no satisfaction in those pairings. It was only when he started bringing the women home, having sex with them in the marital bed, forcing Betty to watch as he fucked other women right in front of her, that he finally felt some degree of satisfaction. He had finally found a way to break her spirit, to hurt her, to make her go against him.

He brought more women home, and Betty was understandably distraught. He slept with them in front of her, two at a time, and she raged against him. Finally, he had what he was looking for. The expression on her face when she realized that she was completely impotent against him. The realization that he meant to go on doing this over and over, right in front of her. The dream of her future was crumbling to dust before her very eyes. Finally, Gary started to feel good.

For the longest time, he continued doing this, because he thought that sleeping with the other women was finally bringing excitement back into his life, but gradually it must have become apparent even to him that the cruelty was the point. It wasn't the fact that he was sleeping with other women that was getting him excited, it was the pain that he was inflicting on his wife.

Once that puzzle piece slotted into place, his affairs came to a halt, and the domestic abuse began to blossom in its place. His wife, already hurt and upset from his actions, had become withdrawn and allowed her work around the household to suffer alongside her. This provided Gary with the ideal opportunity to beat her into compliance. Betty would often be seen with a black eye when the two went out together, but in spite of all the social progress that had been made in the preceding decade, nobody intervened on her behalf. They sometimes ate at the local Franklin Diner, her staring at her feet the whole time, him ordering for the both of them, and many people mistook the situation, thinking that she wasn't fluent enough to interact herself, when in fact she could speak absolutely perfect English. Her anger and resentment towards him also allowed him to feel sexually fulfilled, because where before she had been the very picture of subservience and compliance, she now refused his advances angrily and he got to experience the joy of rape all over again. Rape was perpetrated not against a scared and confused girl with the intellect of a toddler, but against an actual competent woman with the full range of emotions and understanding of what was happening to her. There was nothing in the world that Gary enjoyed more than exerting his "rights" over his wife. No joy to be found in any aspect of it that was greater than the sense of power when he physically forced her to indulge his most disgusting desires.

Outside of sex, servitude, and violence, all of which had gradually blurred together into possession for Gary, the man and his wife had very little interaction with one another. She was free to roam and do as she pleased, so long as her chores were completed, and that gradually led to her making some friends around the neighbourhood. There were plenty of people who had the sense that her relationship with Gary wasn't ideal, and she was soon befriended by several of the women on her street who would try to talk her into leaving him.

Of course, that was easier said than done. She had travelled around the world to be with him, she had married him, which in her mind was still a sacred vow taken before the eyes of God. He controlled all of their finances and was the sole breadwinner, and even if she were to somehow get away from him, she had no skills or prospects that would allow her to support herself. She felt as though she was completely alone in the world, and the situation was only going to get worse.

But there was a light at the end of that tunnel. Through her friends in the neighbourhood, she was put into touch with the Filipino community in Philadelphia, and through them, she had a way out, a way back home to her family. Gary hadn't even considered the possibility that his wife might choose to go back to what he considered to be a third-world country rather than endure his abuse, and Betty was frozen in place herself. Uncertain of what she wanted to do, if she wanted to leave or try to endure just a little longer in the hopes that Gary might improve himself.

That all changed with a visit to the doctor's office. She was no longer only risking her own life by staying with her abusive husband. She was now risking the life of their unborn child. She didn't tell Gary about what she had learned from the doctor, not realizing that she was protected by confidentiality laws, but she did tell all of her friends that she'd discovered she was pregnant with "Little Gary" and that he was still beating her all the same. The consensus opinion of the women of the Filipino community was that if he didn't stop hitting her even when she was pregnant, he would never stop, the only way that she and her child would ever be safe was to get away from him.

Gary returned home one day in 1986 to find his wife gone. All of the clothes he'd bought for her had been packed up in a suitcase and were gone too. The wedding ring that he'd pushed onto her finger in Maryland lay sitting on the kitchen table. There was no trace of her to be found. She had made her escape.

He raged and he cursed, descended into a brief bout of depression so severe that it frightened everyone that knew him, but before long he had found some equilibrium again. This was not the first setback he had ever experienced in his life, and he wouldn't make the same mistakes again. Betty had definitely been a mistake, trusting any woman to be good, Godly, and obedient in the modern age, regardless of where they came from, was clearly too much to ask. If he wanted a woman like that then he was going to have to make one from scratch. Break her down and build her up again from the ground up. It was no great loss. Or at least, so he told himself. She might have been the perfect wife on paper, but she'd never given him what he really wanted.

And so he went on thinking until he received a letter in the mail from the other side of the world. A letter conveyed through a legal firm in the USA. One demanding child support payments from him, for his son Jesse John Disto. It seemed that Betty had decided against naming the child after her rapist and abuser after all.

Gary had gone through a cycle of grief and loss after Betty departed, but now his friends described him as losing his mind entirely. He stopped leaving the house after receiving the news. He began hammering night and day, driving nails through pennies into his kitchen wall. Paranoia, always an undercurrent in him, came to the fore and he became suspicious of everyone and anyone. Needless to say, he stopped taking the medication that he was prescribed, no longer trusting it to help him any more than he trusted in the doctors who hadn't even told him that he had a son on the way.

The son was a great loss for Gary. The first child that he would have been able to keep if it wasn't for that treacherous bitch fleeing the country. A child that would have had his name, his face, his mind. A perfect carbon copy of him that he could have raised up into the first of a perfect new race. He had been robbed once more. Not just of the chance at a normal life, that he could somehow still convince himself that he wanted, but also of the future that he demanded. A future in which he was the father of a dynasty that perfectly blended all the best traits of all races. A brighter, happier future for all mankind, born of his seed.

He had no choice but to pay the child support, but he conferred with his lawyers to make it as difficult as possible for

Betty to receive it, threatening all sorts of legal action if he ever found out that a single penny of his money had been spent on anything other than the boy. It was all just chest-thumping and posturing at this point. There was more than ample evidence of the abuse that he'd inflicted on Betty, and there hadn't even been any attempt to contest the dissolution of their marriage from his end. There was nothing that he could do that wouldn't result in airing all of their dirty laundry publicly and destroying his reputation. He didn't rely on the church financially anymore, but that didn't mean that he was willing to throw away his position of power and moral authority when he didn't have to. It wasn't as though it would have done him any good, even if he had fought. There was no way he could get his child back, they would never separate the brat from his mother, and he certainly wasn't going to be getting Betty back, given the hoops and loops she'd had to jump through to get away from him to begin with. She'd gone from having all the money she could ever need back to outright destitution rather than spend another moment in his company, and in an odd way he ended up admiring that she had the courage of her convictions. He hated her, obviously, more than he had ever hated anyone in his entire life, but that didn't mean that her frantic escape in the dead of night hadn't earned her a little bit of respect. He'd thought of her as a useless and weak creature beneath contempt, and she had used that contempt as a shield to hide her movements until she could make her escape, taking the only thing that Gary had ever cared about with her.

 At this point, Gary was in a spiral. He had girls around the house constantly, working girls that were so obvious about their profession that even the neigbours who had so politely ignored his comings and goings before took note. There was a near-constant stream of shouting emerging from the house, but it seemed to intensify when the prostitutes came around as if he was just banking the fires of his anger throughout every day and only unleashing the full fury of it when they arrived. Often, they'd end up leaving early, in a hurry to get the hell away from him. Other times the fighting would escalate to the point that he physically threw them out of the house. On one occasion the police had to be called because a girl of little more than eighteen years old had been thrown naked out of the house on North Marshall Street and Gary wouldn't let her back in to get her clothes. The police arrived and the matter was handled quietly with Gary handing the clothes out and refusing both the police and the woman access to his home. The officers on the scene shielded the poor girl with their bodies as she got dressed on the porch and then gave her a ride back into the centre of town to get her out of this nice neighbourhood with all the staring eyes peeking out from behind twitching blinds.

Even this wasn't the limit of antisocial behaviours that Gary began to cultivate. Beyond his "home improvements" and various evening visitors, even the people that had once considered him to be a friend started to be disturbed by his behaviour. A car would park outside of his house for too long, and he would shoot out its windows with a BB gun. If that didn't work, he would sneak out under cover of darkness and pour sugar into the gas tank. He didn't want strangers anywhere near to his house and he apparently didn't recognize the dichotomy of expressing that sentiment while simultaneously inviting streetwalkers in on a daily basis.

It was clear that once again, Gary was heading towards a crisis point, and it would arrive sooner than even he could have anticipated. Betty had learned a lot about America during her time there. She had spent time amongst the Filipino community, learned about the laws of the land, and the things that a man could and could not do to his wife without any expectation of repercussions. The only reason that he hadn't yet been arrested was that she wanted to make sure that her filing for child support was processed first, in case his assets were frozen after he was imprisoned. On a pleasant and mild afternoon, a pair of plainclothes detectives arrived at Gary's home, had a civil conversation with him on his doorstep and then he departed with them, without making a scene. He was allowed to get himself organized and tidied up, make a call to his lawyer to meet him down at the station and lock the place up safely.

This time there was none of the preamble from his previous arrest, they had the victim's full statement on what had occurred and all of the evidence that they needed, evidence that had been collected before Betty left the country to avoid suffering repercussions for going against her husband. Where before Gary and his lawyers had been able to manipulate the prosecution with the weakness of their case, this time their case was rock solid. This left only two options. Pursue the mental health defense again, at the risk of permanently damaging Gary's credibility, or accept a plea bargain. Given the quality of his lawyers, the actual sentence that he'd end up serving for his crimes was absolutely tiny in comparison to the list of crimes themselves. Assault, indecent assault, spousal rape, and Gary's favourite crime; involuntary deviant intercourse, yet again. All the grotesque details of the things that he had forced his wife to watch, and the things that he had forced her to participate in, were laid out before him. If the prosecution had expected him to flinch, or show any sort of remorse, then they were mistaken. He did not break down in tears like so many abusers when they were caught out, he knew exactly what he had done to her, and he just did not care. He didn't see her as a person, so why would he care if she was upset by the things that he'd put her through. She existed to serve him, and to produce his babies, and she had not only failed in the former, she had utterly betrayed him when it came time to perform the latter task. She was his enemy, and he felt no shame in having done anything he was accused of to an enemy.

The distressing thing was that in spite of all the progress that society had made in the past couple of decades, there would be plenty of jurors who took the same position as Gary. Betty wouldn't be there to make her case, but the charismatic preacher could take the stand, talk at length about how she had done him wrong, stolen his baby, and blackmailed him for child support. He could have played to the racism of the crowd, the strangeness of the arrangement, framed himself as the victim in the whole thing, and insist that the entire prosecution was just more of the woman's vengeance being brought against him.

Nobody wanted this to go to trial and risk everything coming out. Least of all the prosecutors who could easily see everything turning against them, thanks in no small part to the clever little insinuations that Gary and his highly paid lawyers were making. He accepted a plea deal, serving a few months in a minimum security facility where he'd still have telephone access so that he could manage his investments. It was technically a worse punishment than he'd suffered for abducting and raping a mentally disabled woman, but that was most likely because this time there was actual testimony against him. Also, he wasn't as willing to throw himself to the mercy of the mental health institutions, given how long he might have ended up trapped in there if he had to go through yet more arduous rounds of testing and therapy to try and identify a mental illness that could have caused his behaviour. He'd learned from the last time around that it was only worthwhile to use his status as a mentally ill veteran to get out of jail time if it was liable to last more than three years.

Almost as soon as he was arrested, he was out again. He was on his best behaviour while he was in prison, he had no issues with the guards or the other prisoners; he behaved well and kept tidy, they really had no good reason not to let him out on probation.

In a funny way, Gary's stay in prison actually worked out pretty well for him. It gave him a break from his day-to-day life, so he wasn't constantly being reminded of Betty's betrayal and the son that he'd never get to see. It gave him a holiday from the repetitive tasks that he had set for himself, giving his brain a rest from the monotony of it all and allowing him to think clearly for perhaps the first time in months or years. Everything that usually occupied his mind was gone, and all that remained was him and his thoughts.

His ultimate goal had not changed, it never would change. He wanted to leave behind a legacy. He wanted a sprawling dynasty of children and grandchildren that would carry on his name into eternity. He was well on his way to accumulating a fortune large enough to ensure that every one of his children would have the best start in life, and that combined with a firm belief that his own extraordinary intellect would be granted to all of his descendants led him to believe that the future would be bright for all the little Heidniks that he left behind. The only problem, as he saw it, was that in the process of producing the babies he desired, he often lost control of the situation. Outside interference had robbed him of his babies, time and time again, shuttling them off into care, or to some foreign country. He needed to make sure that nothing like that could happen again. He needed to completely eliminate the possibility of ever losing a baby again. Sitting there in his cell with nothing to do, and nowhere to go, that was where he focused his thoughts. Laying out his plans for what would come next.

The Pit

On his release, Gary began putting all of his newly made plans into motion. He returned to normalcy, in as much as he ever had any normalcy in his life, making regular visits to his parishioners, holding church ceremonies in his home which he had converted into a chapel, taking care of his money, and picking up prostitutes with the same regularity that he always had. It was as if he was trying to make it seem as though nothing had changed in his life. As if he could just ignore his now ex-wife, his stay in prison, and everything else that had occurred. As if, by behaving as though everything was as it should be, he could force reality to align with his twisted vision of the world.

He continued with the home improvements that he'd made after Betty's departure. He finished up his wall of pennies in the kitchen before moving on to the basement, where he began excavation work on the dirt floor. He was careful never to bring any of the dirt up from the basement, as he didn't want any of the damned nosy neigbours to become aware of what he was doing, instead loading it into trash bags, and simply moving it around the room. Before long he had a decent-sized pit opened up and a stack of bags reaching halfway up the wall. That would do the trick.

The rest of what he needed he picked up from a few hardware stores around town, and what he couldn't get from there, he was able to mail-order. Faster than he ever could have believed, he was ready to begin looking for prospects to fill his baby farm. Incubators that he could use to produce his heirs.

On November 25th of 1986, Gary finally put his plan into action. Trawling the streets in his Coupe De Ville Cadillac, looking for a woman that fit his parameters. At the intersection of 3rd Street and Girard, he found her. At about 11 p.m. he picked up a young woman named Josefina Rivera and they took a little drive to discuss some business. He took her on a turn around the block as they discussed the pricing of her services until they came to a mutual agreement that she would accompany him back to his house and perform the deed for the jaw-dropping price of $20. From there, they took a direct route back to his house on North Marshall Street, proceeded inside and headed right upstairs. On the second-floor front bedroom, there was a waterbed. After handing over the twenty, Gary and Josefina carefully removed their clothes, leaving them in a pile in the corner of the room, and proceeded to have sex. None of this was particularly noteworthy for Josefina, who did this sort of thing as many times a night as it was possible for her to do in her pursuit of financial stability.

What made this visit to a strange man's bed notable was that when they were done and she got to her feet to go and get dressed again, she was stopped by hands locked around her throat, choking the breath out of her. She struggled briefly but was unable to draw a single breath and she quickly succumbed to Gary's seemingly lethal grasp on her throat. She fell back onto the bed and into the darkness of unconsciousness for what felt like a mere instant but could have been far longer without her ever knowing.

As she came to, she realized that there was a handcuff around one of her wrists. Josefina opened her mouth to scream, only to find Gary's lethally tight grip around her throat had returned. "If you make a single sound, I'm going to strangle you."

She opened her mouth again, but he barked, "Shut up," and that was exactly what she did. "If you don't shut up and stay shut up, I'm going to choke you out."

"Alright, alright." She had conceded. "I'll do whatever you want, just don't hurt me."

As he led her down into the basement, Josefina tried her best to work out how the hell she was going to get out of this one. Usually, she'd just up and run, but Gary had already gotten ahold of her and choked her out without even breaking a sweat. She couldn't expect any future escape attempts to be any different, and besides, so long as she could keep him calm, she felt as though the danger might pass. This was a false assumption. Gary forced her down the stairs with her hands cuffed in front of her, led her through the lower floor of the house and then continued down into the basement. It took a moment for her eyes to adjust to the darkness, and then she realized just how much trouble she was in. There was a hole in the floor, big enough for a person to fit inside. He'd dug her a grave.

At once she started panicking again, trying to break free of his grasp, but he just held onto the chain linking her wrists together and waited for her initial screaming to come to an end. When she hadn't been murdered by the end of that, she seemed to calm down a little. It was then that he explained to her what was going to happen. She was going to live here with him. If she was well-behaved, she would live upstairs in the house. If she was badly behaved, she would live down here in the basement. For now, she hadn't had any opportunity to prove that she was going to behave herself, so he had to treat her as untrustworthy, which meant that she was going to have to stay here in the basement and be restrained until she had earned his trust.

That all sounded surprisingly reasonable, which in itself was probably just a sign of how bad Josefina's life was outside of this basement. She'd have a roof over her head, food in her belly, and someone to take care of her. She had heard of far worse arrangements, especially for girls like her on the street. As he talked, she fell into an almost hypnotic trance, being taken in by the story that he was weaving about how she would only be down here until he was confident in her, and that he was sure that would happen in no time at all.

As he spoke, he fitted something like shackles around her ankles, she'd later learn that they were a car component meant to hold mufflers in place, but that didn't mean much of anything to her at that moment. They were just the latest in the long line of anxieties that this night was inflicting on her. Once he had them on, he used a nut and bolt to seal them so that they couldn't be removed. Immediately, she started thinking about how she'd get them off.

Once he left, she'd be able to unscrew that nut, slip the bolt out and set herself free, with her legs free, she'd be able to move around the basement as she pleased, and from there she'd just have to get up the stairs and through the door to get back into the house, and then outside. It wouldn't be easy, but this guy clearly had money if he had a car like that, and that meant he had a job to go to. She'd have all day to get out.

He turned his back on her, walking over to a toolbox and fetching out a little tube of Krazy glue. He applied it all around the nut and bolt, waiting until it dried solid, locking the bolt in place so that even with the right tool, Josefina wouldn't have had the strength to break the bond. It was like he'd read her mind. She looked up at him, with the fear really sinking in now, not just the initial panic, but the bone-deep terror of what her future was going to be. And then in her darkest moment when all hope seemed to have been lost, he smiled at her. "I'm going to take care of you."

He took her by the chain between her wrists and led her over to the hole in the ground, carefully helping her in. It wasn't deep enough that it would have been difficult to get into normally, but in chains and shackles, he had to help her down, every step of the way. She shivered every time his hands brushed over her bare skin. He wasn't molesting her by any stretch of the imagination, probably still satisfied after their tumble upstairs, but the way that he touched her still unsettled her. It wasn't like he was a man and she was a woman, but more like he was a man and she was a pet he was checking over for injuries. If he'd pried apart her lips to check her teeth she wouldn't have been surprised. Once she was in the pit, they took a little break, and he explained why he was doing all this. She'd already concocted some fairly terrible reasons for what was happening in her head, so it should have come as a relief to find out what was actually going on, but as he laid out his plans for her, the dread that had already been mounting became an unbearable weight.

He was going to keep her, he was going to rape her, he was going to get her pregnant, and then he was going to raise their baby. Then he was going to do it again, and again, and again, until her body gave out, and she couldn't do it anymore. He hoped that with some time together, she would earn his trust, prove to him that she could be relied on, move upstairs and help with taking care of the babies, like she was his wife, instead of his slave. She tried to imagine what that might be like, that white picket fence life, living like a happily married woman in suburbia. She tried to work out what the best way to play this was, the way that might get her out of there alive. Right now, it was just the two of them, despite his rambling plans for her to have other women down here with her, and while he was obviously crazy, he didn't seem like he could be reasoned with at all. She tried to tell him that she'd be good, that she'd do everything that he wanted of her. It was hardly the first time she'd slept with a guy that scared the hell out of her. She did that almost every night. He'd take her upstairs, she'd do her thing, and then when he was completely exhausted, she could walk right out of the place. If that wasn't going to work, then she could build up his trust, just like he said, and escape during the day when he was out, once she was allowed freedom to move. This wasn't the end for her. She could already see a dozen ways out of this.

That was when he started putting the boards over the top of the hole. They were solid wood, not too heavy, but heavy enough that when he brought one down on her head a little hard she yelped. The pit wasn't deep enough for her to stand upright, or wide enough for her to crouch down, it was just wide enough that when he laid the board on top of her it forced her neck to the side and crushed her. She let out an involuntary yell of pain, and he immediately started hitting her. Tearing the boards away so that he could slap and beat her until she fell silent once more. The next time he was less gentle slamming the boards down on top of her, but she crushed herself down into the pit as best she could, whimpering all the way. With the boards placed over the hole, trapping her beneath the earth, she couldn't see what Gary was doing in the basement above, but she could hear him grunting with effort as he moved something heavy around, something heavy that he then dumped on top of the boards over her head, making them bend down that little bit further to press on her cheek. By now, she had lost her composure, she was weeping and doing her best not to scream, given how that had turned out for her last time. She couldn't breathe. There was no air. She screamed and she screamed, but he didn't let her out. She told him she couldn't breathe. She told him there was no air down there. That she was going to suffocate. That she was going to die. He didn't even answer her.

There was no light down in the pit, the basement was dim enough that what little could have filtered down through the gaps between the boards wasn't noticeable. She was trapped, chained, twisted and contorted, in absolute darkness and mounting pain. She didn't even hear him leaving. Didn't hear him tramping up the steps. All she heard was the click, as he turned out the lightbulb and left her there for the night.

Time lost all meaning in the pit. It was impossible to fully fall asleep with the constant pain of her contorted body, but time still seemed to pass as though she was in a dream. Day and night meant nothing. The passage of time meant nothing. There was just her, down here in the dark and the silence. It was so bad, that when she finally heard the voice of the man who'd imprisoned her at the top of the basement stairs, it was a relief. He brought her water and crackers, and let her out of the hole to move around a little. She was so relieved that she broke down in tears thanking him. She felt pathetic, but she did it all the same. If he could be convinced that she was on his side, if he could be convinced that she could be trusted, he wouldn't need to put her back in the pit. Yet almost as soon as she had finished eating and drinking the meagre rations, that was exactly where he moved to put her. She pleaded with him. She begged. She'd do anything he wanted if it meant she didn't have to go back in the pit. All the services that were usually off the menu when she was prostituting herself had just suddenly become available. But despite having taken his pleasure in her just a day before, it seemed as if now he was a stone wall. He showed no interest in her body whatsoever, even though she was fully naked and offering herself to him. He pushed and pulled her until she was back down in the hole, and when she started screaming, he picked up a whippy length of scrap wood and started beating her around the head with it until she fell silent. Sinking down onto her haunches, she sobbed silent and furious tears as he placed the boards back on top of her pit and abandoned her all over again.

The next day, he didn't bother to visit at all. She had already pissed herself but now had to squat down and empty her bowels in the mud at the bottom of the pit. She wasn't just trapped in there with her own hot breath but with the stench of that too. When he came back the next day, he ran a hose down from the kitchen to clean her off and used a shovel to dig out the hole a little more, including the mess that she'd made. She sat against the wall while he worked, quaking and shivering until, apparently as an afterthought, he gave her a dry turkey sandwich and wished her a happy Thanksgiving. She was hungry enough that she couldn't even laugh at the irony of the situation, just scrabbling the food down as fast as she possibly could. She probably should have used the opportunity to try and make a run up the stairs, she could see the door was still unlocked and this could have been her best chance to escape, but the sad truth was that she was too sore, tired and weak to run after the last 48 hours. When he put her back into the pit, she actually felt grateful that he'd dug it out a little bit deeper and given her a little more room. She could stand now. Only barely. With food inside her, it felt like her brain was starting to turn over again. If it was Thanksgiving today, that meant she'd been down in the basement for three days in total. Three days with only a few crackers, water, and a single sandwich for sustenance, it was no surprise that she felt so weak already. She hadn't missed an opportunity to escape, no matter how much she was inclined to beat herself up over what had happened. This had been planned, just like the glue on her shackles. This Gary guy had worked out exactly what to do to make it so she couldn't escape. Given enough time, he'd make mistakes, he'd slip up, and there would be a way out of this, but for now, there was nothing to do except go on trying to survive.

Sandra Lindsay knew Gary for about four years before her abduction. She was a twenty-five-year-old woman who sporadically attended his church, but much more frequently attended the local McDonalds restaurant where he would buy meals for her and her friends. She was mentally disabled, like the vast majority of the girls that he had "dated" in the past, and he had discussed the possibility of her living with him and having his babies for him many times in the past, with her getting cold feet each time. He was a nice man, in her estimation, but her ability to judge such things was extremely limited, and he was so far beyond the limit of anything that she might have imagined that he might as well have been invisible.

The day after Thanksgiving, her period was about to start, and she was suffering from cramps. They didn't have any pain medication in the house, so Sandy announced to all and sundry that she was going to the pharmacy to pick some up. It was a relatively long walk to the drug store from where she lived and she was in pain, so when a friendly face pulled up in a car beside her and offered her a lift, she obviously said yes.

Sandy was completely open about why she was out and about, and Gary was quick to promise her pain relief that would go well beyond what the pharmacy could offer. He had pills at home that would sort her right out. She gladly went along with him to his house. When he tried to bring her down to the basement, she finally realized that something wasn't quite right, but she didn't have the wherewithal to realize just how dangerous her situation was. "It's okay." He told her, talking loudly over her increasingly frantic complaints. "Be quiet. Shut up Sandy, you know I'm not going to hurt you."

When they came down the stairs into the basement, Josefina immediately started shouting from down in the pit. That startled Sandy all over again, but then childish curiosity won out. Was it some sort of game? Was it a surprise party? Where was the person shouting from? She hurried down the stairs, face alight with excitement, only to find the empty basement. Gary carefully locked the door behind him, then came down to uncover Josefina where she was down in her hole.

"What is this?" She laughed in confusion. Why was there a naked lady here? That was so silly. "You're so silly."

Gary was smiling, like it was all some big joke, but the lady in the hole, she wasn't smiling at all. She looked scared. She looked sad. She looked like all the feelings that Sandy never wanted to feel. Gary laid it all out for her, as plain as he could. Nice and simple, so that even she could understand. Her job was to have babies. That was what all women's real job was. She was going to be living here with him and doing that job. They were going to be a mommy and a daddy. Sandy understood this well enough, she had already made promises to Gary to this effect in spite of having little understanding of the mechanics involved. But who was this other lady?

"This is Jo. She's going to be doing the same job as you. You're both going to live here together. It will be like you're sisters."

Josefina had frozen up. One part of her wanted to scream at this poor girl, tell her to run for her life, but that part of her was silenced by the larger part of her that wanted to get out of this alive. If there were two of them down here, they had better chances of overpowering Gary. If there were two of them down here, then whatever punishments Gary decided to dole out would be split between them instead of all falling solely on Josefina. Not to mention that when Gary got a little frisky, there would be twice as many targets for him to hit, so she was halving the number of times she was going to have to endure his touch. The last thought was not a kind one, she wouldn't have willingly consigned another woman to be raped if she actually had any say in the matter, but the truth was that she had no strength to do much of anything right now, and she was still in fear for her life, no matter how she tried to convince herself that she could see ways out of this.

Sandy had gone on trying to talk her way out of the basement, as if she had any hope of outwitting Gary. "It's only one mommy and one daddy to make a baby."

"But we aren't just making one baby, Sandy. We've got to make lots of them. You see, in the future, there aren't going to be white people and black people and Asian people, they're all just going to be one people. All mixed together, and all living in peace for the first time in history. And we're going to start that here. You and me, and Jo. We're going to start making a new world."

"But I don't know..."

Gary pressed a beatific kiss on her forehead, "My sweet girl, you don't need to know. I know. I know everything that we need to know. All you have to do is trust in me."

The process of getting Sandy out of her clothes and into her chains was a prolonged one, punctuated by her letting out startled cries and trying to cover her body with her hands. She knew, in the abstract, that nobody was meant to see certain parts of her, that they were shameful and had to be hidden. And though Gary laid on his calming voice and laid out the many reasons that everything was absolutely fine and that God approved of what they were doing, she still couldn't overcome that shame.

Every time that Jo managed to work up the courage to call out and tell the girl she was right, that she should run, that she should get away from here and get help, Gary seemed to sense it. He'd turn that baleful gaze on her and she'd fall silent. All through the painstaking progress of the work, affixing the chains and the clamps and the bolts and the glue, there were so many times she could have tried to stop it, so many times that she should have stopped it. But she never found the courage to go against Gary.

With the two of them bound, Jo fully expected to be returned to the pit, but it seemed that now that they had company, Gary meant to show off. They could all spend time in each other's company, and even when Gary went upstairs to use the bathroom, he left the two of them with the freedom to roam the basement. Jo lurched into motion the second he was out of sight, looking through the shelves, trying to find something, anything that might help them get out of this situation. There had been a toolbox, she was sure of it, that was where Gary had gotten the glue when he put her in the pit for the first time, but now it was gone. Everything that might have been useful in an escape attempt was gone. Even the shelves themselves had been bolted and glued too tight for them to be pried apart and used. There was nothing down there that Jo could use to enact her escape plan, except for Sandy.

The girl had just watched the other woman shuffling back and forth, frantically trying to solve some puzzle that she wasn't even aware of, but now she rushed up to her, she took hold of her hands and she held on tight, even though Sandy was trying to pull her hands away. "We're going to be alright. We're going to get out of this. You've just got to hold on, okay? You've just got to stay strong."

Gary came back downstairs, and the woman went back to doing nothing at all, acting as if she had never come anywhere near Sandy. Sandy was already so confused before they even began that this latest contradiction didn't mean a thing to her. She had no idea what was happening, she had no idea what this Jo woman was trying to tell her, or why she was behaving so strangely. Now that Sandy was getting accustomed to her nudity, she was barely worried at all. Gary gave them some food and some water, and when Sandy asked for soda, he said he didn't have any. Then it was bedtime, so he told them to get comfortable and left them down there.

It was the first time that Jo hadn't been confined to the pit, the first night since her abduction that she'd been able to actually lie down, and with the veritable feast of leftovers that Gary had brought down for the two of them, she had a full enough stomach that she wasn't curling around it in pain. She should have been using this brief period of strength and lucidity to work on her escape, but her exhaustion after so many sleepless nights and days sapped her of her will to fight so she settled down to sleep on the dirt floor, and it felt as comfortable as a goose down mattress after so long without being able to lie down at all. Almost the moment she laid down, she faded.

Sandy, on the other hand, had no exhaustion to drag her down into a dreamless sleep. She lay down because it seemed to be what was expected of her, but she couldn't settle in such a strange place with such a strange person lying just a short distance away. Her mommy was going to be worried about her. Her sister too. She hadn't told them she was going away. She'd only told them she was going to the drugstore. They were going to be scared when she didn't come home.

Tracey Lomax, Sandy's sister, was exactly as worried as the situation warranted almost immediately. She went out searching for her sister just an hour after she'd departed from the home and then enlisted everyone in her neighbourhood to help with the search when there was no sign of her between the drug store and home. They searched the entirety of the neighbourhood for any sign of the girl and came up with nothing. They spoke to everyone who was around, but there had been no sightings. Over the course of the weekend, the family and their friends combed through the whole city, starting from Sandy's favourite places and working out from there, as Sandy and Tracey's mother became increasingly overwrought with emotion.

By Monday, the panic had turned into a terrible certainty that something bad had happened to the girl. She had been known to wander off on occasion, but not for this long, and not without even calling home. Sandy loved to use the phone at any opportunity, even when she had nothing to say. There was no way that she would have gone somewhere and not even called. Tracey and her mother went down to the police station to report the girl going missing and encountered the biggest impediment to her safety other than her kidnapper, Detective Julius Armstrong.

Armstrong did not grasp the issue with Sandy's absence. She was twenty-five years old, an adult in the eyes of the law, and despite her being mentally disabled, she was capable of holding down a job. In his eyes, this was just an overprotective parent freaking out over nothing, despite the details of the girl's absence. He wasn't going to do anything.

Tracey took matters into her own hands. They hadn't heard from Sandy's friend Tony since her disappearance, even though they typically spent a lot of their time together, and he likely would have noticed her absence too. So the next step in their plan to track her down was to find him. They staked out the local McDonalds to wait for him, and within an hour or two, he showed up. Tony was a member of Gary's church, and he knew that the man had taken an interest in Sandy, so he passed the man's number on to Tracey and her mother. They called him. "Gary, where's Sandy?"

There was a long pause, and then Gary simply replied. "No. Not here." Then he hung up on them.

It was suspicious enough that they made their way over to his house, and even though he wouldn't answer the door, that didn't mean that their search was over. Questioning his neigbours and showing a picture of Sandy to them. One of the women who had become increasingly aware of Gary's strangeness and tried to keep an eye on him confirmed that she had seen Sandy going into the house recently. Surely that was enough to get the police involved. Tracey took that information back to Detective Armstrong and forced his hand. He got out from behind his desk, took a car from the pool down to Gary's house, knocked on the door, got no reply, and posted a card through the door for anyone named Gary at that address to contact the West Philadelphia Detectives Bureau. There was no response to that card.

Instead, there was a Christmas card with $20 inside, written and signed by Sandy, and postmarked from New York, delivered to her family on Christmas Eve. To the police, that marked the end of the period of suspicion, a clear sign that Sandy had simply moved on with her life. To her family, it was a clear sign that something terrible had happened. Sandy never wrote if given the choice, she was terrible at it and hated doing it. The fact that they'd received a card rather than a phone call suggested something very strange was going on.

In truth, Gary had, of course, organized the whole thing. Making sure to wear gloves while handling both the money and the card and ensuring that Sandy's own fingerprints were all over both and then confining both of the girls to the pit so that he could make a drive up to New York and post the letter from there. He was not going to be caught out again like he had been the last time he attempted this experiment, he had thought everything through and planned everything ahead. He would extract the information required from the girls as necessary to convince anyone who had come looking for them that they were not coming back. It would be so simple, given the complete control that he had over them.

Of course, while the police and Sandy's family had been making their clumsy attempts at an investigation into the disappearances that had already occurred, Gary was out making more of them happen. His plan was grandiose, with his intention of ten brood mares kept in his basement always at the forefront of his mind.

He picked up Lisa Thomas at the junction of 6th and Lycoming, a few days before Christmas, just after his trip to New York. From there, they moved on to City Line Avenue, where they went into a TGI Fridays for some lunch. Lisa got a cheeseburger and fries, while Gary sneered at the menu offerings and eventually settled on a Martini. After she'd eaten, he took her to the fanciest store he could think of, Sears and Roebucks, and offered to buy her anything that she wanted. With the caveat that it couldn't cost more than $50. Even with that slight damper on things, it was still one of the better dates that Lisa had been on recently, and despite being a little older, this Gary guy really seemed to have his life together. He could talk with her forever about anything that she wanted, without ever seeming to get bored, and unlike most guys, it was obvious that he was really paying attention to what she said, because he'd make little references to earlier parts of their conversation, sometimes as jokes, sometimes as just little offhand comments about something that she was saying. He seemed to be really interested in her as a person, and that was the kind of thing that was hard to fake. So, when the time came that he invited her back to his house to have a beer and "hang out" some more, she had no intention of saying no.

They arrived at his place on Marshall Street, had that promised beer in the living room, and then headed up the stairs to the front-facing bedroom where he'd taken Jo before her. The two of them had sex on his waterbed, but at the very moment that activity came to its conclusion, he locked his hands around her neck, nearly choking the life out of her. She pleaded and begged him not to hurt her, and said that he could do anything that he wanted with her.

That was precisely what he did. He produced the handcuffs from under the bed, and locked her wrists together, then took her downstairs to the basement. In the pit, beneath the boards, the other women cried out as she arrived. Begging for food, begging to be let out. They had lost all trace of dignity by this point in their confinement, and if they thought that begging Gary for something might help their situation, then that was exactly what they would do. Survival was all that mattered. Dignity and self-respect could come later, after they'd escaped. It was hard to feel any sort of dignity when you spent your time in a hole in the ground, soaking your feet in your own piss.

He removed the boards, letting Lisa see what her future was going to hold, and set to work fitting her with the same muffler-fitting shackles that the other two already wore. He had learned from his mistakes with the previous two. He gave her a length of chain between her shackles much longer than theirs had been. Long enough that she could spread her legs for him without having to remove them. The bolts were glued in place, and he moved on to explaining her situation. The others would have their leg shackles changed to similar-length chains later that same week.

The diet of the women in the basement was typically horrific. They would sometimes be fed nothing but crackers. Sometimes they'd receive hot dogs and rice. Often, they were given stale bread. But the most common food that they were served was dog food that Gary called stew. Both Lisa and Jo were aware of what was being served to them but given that there was actually a decent amount of protein in it compared to the starvation scraps that they'd been living on, they ate it without complaint. Sandy, meanwhile, seemed to be blissfully unaware that there was anything wrong with the food at all.

As a special treat on Christmas day, Gary brought down a Chinese Takeout menu and let each of them order whatever they wanted. It was a small kindness, but in a place with no kindness at all, it was the sort of thing that was very easy to latch onto. By the 26th of December, they were back to dog food.

On New Year's Day, the girls were all out of the pit and relaxing in the basement when Gary arrived with his latest acquisition, Debbie. Where the others had been terrified into compliance by the brief display of brutality after their initial encounter with Gary, the same could not be said for her. She had already lived a life where brutal violence was commonplace, and she was not so easily cowed. He had her cuffed, shackled and in the hole, but still, she wouldn't stop screaming. It went on and on into the night, her constant screeching for help. The other women wanted nothing to do with her, they pressed themselves against the sides of the pit to get away from her. To make sure that when Gary arrived, they couldn't be mistaken for co-conspirators.

It didn't take long for him to tire of the caterwauling. He had two sticks that he used to beat the girls. One of them was just a whippy length of scrap wood, the other a more solid piece with some nails driven through it. It was this second one that he used on Debbie, smacking her across the ass and the backs of her thighs until there were gouges all over and she was bleeding profusely. Only then did he return her to the pit. She was definitely quieter after that. Not as silent as the others had learned to be, but quieter than she had been.

The girls in the basement soon lost all track of time, as there were no clocks, no windows, and no real indication of what was going on outside of the room. Gary kept such irregular hours that they couldn't rely on his sporadic visits to keep track of anything, and they were all so hungry all the time that trying to gauge how much time had passed since their last meal became impossible.

Jacquelyn Askins was the next to arrive. He picked her up off the street on January 18th, a date that it was only possible to ascertain because it was the day before Jo's birthday, and Gary had promised the girls a cake to celebrate. She was a prostitute, like Jo and Debbie before her, and went by the name Donna to try and keep her working and personal lives separate. Gary and the girls would only ever know her as Donna. She came back to the house with cash in her pocket for half an hour's services and then sat in the living room with Gary for a half hour as he played Mr. Do on his Super Nintendo, chatting with her casually. She didn't know what to make of it, but she'd been paid for the time, so she was in no rush to head out. She figured that eventually this weird guy would get over his nerves and they'd get to business, and this was a comfier place to hang out than on some street corner anyway.

When he got tired of his game, he finally turned his attention to "Donna" rising from the sofa and padding over to her with a smile on his face. This felt more familiar to her, she was ready for this sort of behaviour. What she was not ready for was the headlock he abruptly threw her into. She struggled, but that just made him tighten his grip around her neck until she was almost blacking out. She slapped helplessly in his arms as he led her around the house like she was some sort of beast of burden, then took her down the stairs.

In the basement, there were already four naked women waiting and chained. Soon to be five. Donna had fought back as best she could until that moment, but seeing the other four, the fight almost immediately left her. This wasn't just some rough trade, this was a monster wearing a man's skin, and she had no idea how to respond to that. She joined the others in chains.

Dog Food

At this point, with the latest of his acquisitions safely stowed away, Gary began working on the next stage of his plan, but once again, he had not been idle in the time between abductions.

The first and most important thing that he had been doing throughout the whole time that he held the women captive, was raping them. In the beginning, he would rape one a day, before moving on to the next, but he gradually became bored with that and started having sex with several of them at the same time, sometimes working his way through all five women before he was finally done. He tried to ensure that he finished with a different woman each time, to maximize the chances of pregnancy for each of them, but his attention to detail tended to slip a little during those encounters, so he was less than accurate in the division of his labours. These rapes were the entire purpose of abducting these women. To turn them into breeders for his next generation of Heidnik children. The fact that it also crushed their spirits and made them more compliant was just a happy coincidence.

To the end of ensuring their compliance, and to make sure that they could never unite against him, Gary also began giving preferential treatment to the women who were the most obedient, to the women who helped him to manage the others. Almost immediately that was Josefina. She helped corral the other women back into the pit in exchange for being allowed to sleep outside of it, she got them to obey his barked orders with soft words and encouragement. She immediately recognized that there was going to be a hierarchy among them and set herself to work climbing the ranks with all haste.

There was always going to be disobedience among the women, anyone imprisoned naturally pushes back against their oppressors. That pushback required punishment, which Gary was more than willing to dole out but was absolutely delighted to discover that he could have the women dole out amongst themselves. The same stick that had been used to beat Josefina on her arrival in the dungeon was now in her hands, and she used it readily on the other girls. Even among the lower-ranking women, there was violence in service of the will of Gary. There was no misstep too small for another woman to turn on her. No petty complaint that couldn't be taken to Gary in exchange for punishment for the accused and a slight raising of the snitch's rank. It went around and around like that throughout their stay in the basement, with each one of the women slowly learning that they could spend an afternoon upstairs in the house, eat a real meal or even be spared the horrors of sleeping in the pit if they were good and obedient. Each one of them stabbing the others in the back at every opportunity.

Of course, that was not the only violence being done to them, beyond the rapes and the beatings that they received, there was also the matter of the congregation. Despite having his victims trapped in his basement under lock and key, Gary never stopped conducting his weekly sermons in what used to be his dining room. Every Sunday the whole house would be filled with the sound of stomping feet as the congregants came in, and then with the sounds of singing and rejoicing as he led them in their prayers. There was nothing that he could do to soundproof the basement, or at least nothing that could be achieved without a work crew and a hefty investment. If the women down in the basement heard the congregation coming in, the only thing holding them back from crying out for help and bringing the whole house of cards crashing down around Gary's ears was the fear that he had instilled in them. But that was a dangerous tightrope to walk. If he didn't make them scared enough of him, then they would call out for help, if he made them too afraid of him, then they might consider calling out for help to be their only option for survival. The margin of error was too tight, it was a bad investment. So Gary did what he always did, he looked at the problem, turned it on its head, and made a simple plan. The problem was not the congregation upstairs becoming aware of the women below the floor, the problem was the women down in the pit becoming aware of the congregants above. If they didn't hear people coming in, they would not know when to cry out, and they dared not cry out if there was nobody there because they knew it would incur his righteous fury. He could not deafen his parishioners to their cries, but he could deafen the women trapped in his basement. Jo had more than earned her place as his favourite by this point, he trusted her enough that she lived upstairs for the majority of the time, and rarely if ever was consigned to the pit overnight. She was spared the sting of the screwdriver that he drove into the ears of the other girls.

    He started with a small one, taking care not to go too deep in case he killed them, but after a great deal of bleeding that had nothing to do with punctured eardrums, he switched to a larger one, driving it home into the ears of each of the women in turn as they screamed and begged him not to until he learned to use a gag. The ones who had screamed received a beating for their trouble to encourage the others to endure the pain in silence. It was not successful, they all screamed and wept as one of their senses was taken from them in the most brutal way imaginable. Yet, it was a success. Nobody who attended Gary's church ever became aware of their presence.

The problem child of the women was actually the one that Gary had spent years grooming and planning to impregnate, Sandy. She was the one to most often be on the business end of the spiked stick. The one least capable of adapting to her new reality and understanding what was going on. She also had underlying disabilities that Gary had never cared enough to learn about, and they were beginning to affect her health. In February, this came to a head. While all the other women would swiftly gulp down whatever food was given to them, Sandy was slow and sluggish because of a developmental problem with her jaw. Everyone else had already finished their meal, and Gary was becoming frustrated with how long it was taking her to eat the bread that she'd been given. He picked up the stick without the nails driven through it and began to strike her over the back of the head. Again and again. Yelling at her all the while to hurry up. This inevitably upset the girl and led to her sobbing and wailing all the way through trying to force the rest of her food down. She inevitably failed to finish in time, then made the greater mistake of trying to hold onto her tiny scrap of a meal when Gary tried to snatch it away. He could not tolerate any disobedience if he wanted this little experiment to work. She had to be made compliant, or through using her as an example, all the other girls had to be shown what would happen if they misbehaved. Taking her by the handcuffs, he led her over to one of the pine beams that supported the floor above and hooked the chain between her wrists onto it. She had to stand on her tiptoes or risk her shoulders being pulled out of their sockets, and she wailed and wept all the more until Jo stepped up and beat her some more, and then she finally fell into a sniveling silence. If anyone had bothered to check on her, they likely would have discovered that the reason she was being so non-compliant was that she was running a high fever that was resulting in her already developmentally challenged mind running even slower than normal. It was for that very same reason that after only a few hours of hanging there, she began to lose consciousness despite her extreme discomfort. The others had been returned to the pit, Jo had returned upstairs with Gary, Sandy was entirely alone in the dark of the basement. She drifted in and out, feet slipping out from underneath her. Exhaustion and pain fighting within her for victory. Eventually, exhaustion did win, but that was only because she was left hanging there like a helpless mannequin for three days.

When someone is hung by their arms like that, and they fall unconscious, the weight of their own head falling forward can cut off the air supply to their brain. If they are healthy and strong, this usually prompts them to wake up, correct their position and survive, but after months of confinement and starvation, Sandra was neither of those things.

On the morning of the third day, Sandra had stopped moving entirely. Gary shouted at her to wake up, to stop being so lazy, to get moving and he'd let her down, but no response came. Disgusted with her slovenly behaviour, he sent Jo down to hit her in the face, but when the blow made contact, she realized that Sandy's skin was cold. She wasn't playing dead. She was dead.

A silence fell over the basement, a mounting sense of horror at what had occurred made worse when Gary very deliberately lifted the boards off the hole in the ground and let the others out so that they could see her. Some of them wept, some managed to maintain the blank stares that had become their most common expression, but he made sure that all of them understood what they were seeing. One of them was dead. Sandy had defied him, and now she was dead. That was the only lesson he needed them to take away from the sight before them. With Jo's help, he took the body down and carried it upstairs.

With that done, she was sent back to the basement, so that he could think about what to do next in peace. Or, more realistically, so he could panic without spoiling the impression of perfect control that he always maintained while in the presence of the women. He had never expected one of them to die, he hadn't even considered what the hell he was going to do in this situation. The only thing that he knew with certainty was that if he tried to take the body out of here, day or night, he would be spotted by the nosy neigbours, reported to the police, and his world would come crumbling down. He needed a solution, he needed to turn the problem on its head, the way he always had before. That was the core of his genius, taking what others thought of as a crisis and making it an opportunity. It was what had made his fortune. What if this wasn't a problem? What if this was actually a solution to another problem that he was already having? The body was laid out on his kitchen table, an unpleasant smell already beginning to emanate from it.

What he had here was not a dead woman, or evidence of his crimes. What he had here was meat. Bad meat that he wouldn't eat himself, but the sort of thing that you could feed to a dog, certainly. He had a need for dog food. All that he'd have to do was process it.

In the days that followed, a foul smell spread throughout the house, clinging most strongly to Gary when he descended into the basement to have his way with the women and making them gag and retch. There was also the intermittent sound of an electric saw upstairs. One of the many tools that had been removed from the basement before the arrival of the women.

The smell did not go unnoticed by those nosy neigbours that he was so concerned about. A woman by the name of Doris Zubulka was so horrified by the stench spreading out from Gary's house that she confronted him about it. He looked nonplussed, claiming that he'd been cooking and maybe she just didn't like the smell of what he'd made.

Her father also lived on the street, and he was eventually so disgusted by the smell that he called the police. Officer Julio Aponte, a somewhat elderly officer, arrived at the scene and met up with Doris, who described the smell to him as being like burning flesh. He sniffed at the air, but couldn't identify the smell. Still, it was obvious where it was coming from. He approached Gary's door and knocked. He continued to knock on the door for ten minutes without an answer, before entering the rear garden of the property and peering in through the sliding doors into the kitchen, where he saw a large pot boiling over on the stove. The smell was much stronger at the rear of the house, and so overwhelming that Aponte was about to radio in for his supervisor when suddenly Gary came bursting out of the house looking confused at the delegation of police and neigbours camped out on his doorstep.

Before anyone else could get a word in, Doris strode up to him and demanded answers. "Gary, what is that god-awful smell? What's burning?!"

Gary's eyes flitted from her to the cop and her father, then he had the good grace to look embarrassed. "I'm sorry. I was cooking a roast and I fell asleep, it's burned up pretty badly."

Everyone immediately seemed to relax. It was a simple lie, one that made him look foolish, so easy to believe in. Nobody ever lied to make themselves look worse.

Back in the basement, the sudden death of one of their number had changed the women. For Josefina, it had steeled her resolve to escape, but for the others it had led to rising panic. Debbie in particular seemed to have entirely lost all of her self-control with the death of Sandy. She spoke back to Gary. Argued with the other women. She was past the edge of sanity and well on her way to a complete breakdown. After a few days of that, Gary had endured enough. He left the other women in the basement and took Debbie upstairs to "explain a few things to her." When she returned, she was essentially catatonic, back to complete and slavish obedience to everything that Gary said.

It would take the other women days to coax answers out of her about what had happened up there, and when they got those answers, they certainly did not make anyone happy.

What she had seen was so gruesome a sight that even someone who had lived a hard life on the streets was still shaken by it. Sandy's severed head was being boiled in a pot. Her ribs were in a casserole. Her limbs were in the freezer, alongside

Tupperware containers full of the "dog food" that they had all been eating since her death. That was sufficient to buy him the silence that he desired for the foreseeable future.

They ate her remains for over a month because there was nothing else for them to eat. All that Gary offered to them was the cooked-up corpse of their friend and the odd crackers, rice or pop-tarts that he sometimes brought down on those days that he didn't intend to feed them properly. Their choices were to eat what remained of Sandy or to starve to death. Or to refuse the food, anger their captor, and face a far quicker death at his hands.

On March 18th, the quiet before the storm came to an end. Gary had left the girls loose in the basement while he went out, trusting that their good behaviour would continue, and upon his return, he was genuinely shocked to discover that it hadn't. There was unmistakable screaming coming from down below. Storming through the house, he met Jo by the basement door, she was already apologizing frantically, trying to make sure that he knew it wasn't her fault, but he was already well past that. Snatching up a hose, he connected it to the kitchen tap and brought it down to the basement. The women were in the pit, screaming at the top of their lungs, but all it took was for Gary ripping one of the boards away for three of them to fall silent. Only Debbie went on yelling at the top of her lungs, even as Jo turned on the tap upstairs and the pit began to flood.

The girls were all slipping and sliding over one another, trying to climb out, screaming the whole time that the pit was filling up with muddy water, but Gary wasn't even close to done yet. He strode over to the wall and ripped a power socket off, plucking the wires inside and dragging them out. Crouching down by the side of the pool, he touched the live wires to Lisa's chains, electrifying her, and setting her off screaming her lungs out. From there he moved on to the other girls, shocking them one by one until they fell silent and promised that they would stay silent. All of them, except for Debbie. She hadn't stopped screaming for help throughout the entire ordeal, pausing only when the current was running through her, and she physically couldn't do anything except convulse. He told her to shut up, but she wouldn't. He told her that he was going to go on torturing her until she stopped making that damned noise, but she wouldn't. She had passed the point of no return. The point where she'd realized that compliance was just going to get them all killed, the same as Sandy had been. He shocked her again and again. Handing off the duty to Josefina as he hauled the other girls out of the water, but still, Debbie just would not stop. Disgusted, he took the wires out of Jo's shaking hands and held them to the metal looped around Debbie's wrists again, holding them there as she jerked and struggled for over a minute. Finally after so long that all the other girls had fallen into a state of near catatonic stupor, he took the wires away. Debbie's dead body slumped down into the water. Completely immobile. As if she were a puppet that had its strings cut.

He looked at her, sunk just below the surface of the water. He stared down into the pit that he had dug. He stared at the dead woman he had just made. Then he sent Josefina upstairs to fetch down a pad of paper and a pen.

He wrote out a confession to the crime, stating that he and Josefina had electrocuted Deborah Dudley in the basement of 3520 North Marshall Street. He signed it first, then had Josefina sign it, not just as someone involved, but also, bizarrely, as a witness to her own confession. With that done Josefina and Gary dragged the body out of the water and up the stairs.

With the confession signed, he felt that Jo was as culpable for the murder as he was and that he could rely on her to obey his every command because if he went down, she would go down with him.

On a few occasions before, he had taken Josefina outside of the house with him – for instance after the incident with the officer poking around in the back garden he had taken her along with him to play wife when he was making inquiries into getting a high fence erected around their back yard – but this was the first time that he took her out into the car with such a care-free attitude. He drove them to the Burlington Flea Market, where he picked up a map of New Jersey, and from there headed out in that direction. Eventually, they came upon what seemed to be a dirt track and stopped. They walked along a distance into what Josefina assumed was some sort of national park, and then Gary nodded his head. This was where they were going to dump the body.

Despite having his plans for its disposal made, Gary still set about breaking down Debbie's remains when they got back to the house, carefully removing those parts of the body that would help a medical examiner identify it.

Things were no longer going according to plan for Gary, but he was ever the optimist. He now felt that he had something better than psychological dominance to hold over Josefina in the form of the signed confession that he had stored away in his safe; it was time for him to start exploiting that new resource.

Bad Investment

On March 24th, 1987, Gary and Josefina loaded the other girls into the pit in the basement, got into the car and went out hunting. Josefina knew most of the other working girls in the city, either directly or through friends of friends, and Gary couldn't have asked for a more capable wingman in his hunt to replace the two women that he'd lost from his harem.

As they were travelling down Girard Street, Jo spotted a girl that she knew named Agnes Adams. She was exactly Gary's type, and more importantly, Josefina already knew her well enough that the two of them trusted each other implicitly. A trust that she was about to betray. Gary stayed in the car as Josefina got out, walked up to Agnes and talked her into coming back to the house on North Marshall Street with them.

Josefina sat at the dining table as Gary took Agnes upstairs, had sex with her, choked her, cuffed her, and then led her down to the basement. It all happened so fast, and so smoothly, that Jo barely even had time to feel bad about handing another girl over to this monster. If that was the price for his complete trust, then she was willing to pay it. She would have paid much more if it meant that she could get out of this place.

With Agnes safely stowed away with the others, shackled and chained in the basement, Gary returned to Josefina with a wide grin on his face at how well everything had gone. He was euphoric at how simple everything had now become for him. His goal of ten girls had never been more achievable than in that moment. They left the house again, leaving the girls in the basement to teach Agnes the ropes while they headed out to pick up yet another girl. To replace, in a single day, both of the women he'd lost.

Gary was making promises now. Telling Josefina about all of the incredible new treats that he had in store for her, all the special treatment that she'd get now that she was behaving like a proper wife. He'd even let her phone up her family if she wanted. When they came to the junction of 6th and Girard, Josefina told him to pull into the gas station. She knew a girl that lived just along the way, but if she showed up on her doorstep with a guy, it would freak her out. All Gary had to do was wait here, and she'd go fetch her.

He looked Josefina in the eyes, took his measure of her then nodded. "Yeah, you've earned my trust."

From the gas station, Josefina walked, and then, once she was sure she was out of sight, broke into a run. She made it all the way home, where her boyfriend opened the door to her in abject amazement. He had no idea where she'd disappeared to. Assumed that she'd up and left him, moved somewhere new. When she told him about what had happened to her, about the basement and the other women and the torture that she had endured, he didn't believe a word. He said she was crazy, assuming that she'd been off on a bender or hooked on some drug that they'd never taken together. Frustrated and disgusted, she left the apartment, went down to a payphone and called 911.

The story that she told to the operator seemed far-fetched, but they sent a police car down to pick her up and take her statement all the same, if only so they could bust her for making a prank call. On arrival, the officers took in how emaciated she looked, and didn't immediately jump to believing the story about a kidnapping and a rape dungeon, but then they saw the shackle marks on her legs. She told them where Gary was. She told them that if they looked in his house, they'd find naked women chained up in the basement, and a dead body.

Still not entirely convinced, they nonetheless drove along to the petrol station and discovered Gary in his Cadillac, exactly as the woman had described. Officers Savidge and Cannon took him into custody with the intention of questioning him and seeing if any part of the woman's story was true, but he immediately demanded his lawyer. That struck them as odd.

From there, Officer Savidge took Gary to the station, while Officer Cannon and Lieutenant Hansen went along with Josefina to the house. No warrant was required, since she had the keys to the place and allegedly lived there, albeit under absolutely horrific circumstances, if she was to be believed.

The house itself was strangely intimidating with reinforced metal doors and bars on most of the windows. A crucifix was tucked in amongst the bars, to mark the place as a church, but it was easy to overlook. Heading inside there was a deafening blare from a television that had been left on at a high volume, presumably to drown out any other sounds that might have been made. Down in the basement, they found exactly what Josefina had told them that they would. Naked and bound, the women began wailing and crying at the sight of their uniforms, falling to their knees and blessing them for the rescue. As Officer Cannon called for backup and tried to calm the women, the lieutenant headed straight back up to the kitchen and pulled open the freezer. There were body parts still inside. Some were no longer recognizable as human, but most appeared close enough to a human that they no longer had any reason to doubt a single word that Jo had said. The lieutenant left the scene as the other patrol cars arrived, heading for the nearest fire station, where he retrieved bolt cutters and then headed back to the house to cut the women free of their bonds. One by one, they were released, wrapped up in blankets and taken out of the basement that had been their own personal hell. Finally, their nightmare was over.

It was only then that the officers realized that the stove was turned on, and that in a pot, Debbie's head was still on a slow boil.

Gary was arrested and waited patiently for the arrival of his lawyers, refusing to say a single word to the police without them. It would have been for the best if he had maintained that level of silence throughout his journey through the criminal justice system, but it seemed that he did not have that much good sense.

At his arraignment, he claimed that the women in his basement had been there when he moved in. A very easily disproven claim, given the dates involved and how ridiculous a statement it was. In April, shortly after his arraignment, Gary attempted to hang himself in his jail cell. The suicide attempt, like all of the ones he had made before, was unsuccessful. If it was intended to prove that he was insane, along with all the nonsensical statements he had made, he would be gravely disappointed in its effectiveness.

His lawyers pursued an insanity defense, relying on his medical discharge from the army, his bizarre behaviour observed throughout his custody, the long history of time in mental institutions and the bizarre behaviour that underlay the crimes themselves. The prosecution tore those claims of insanity apart. They brought in people from every aspect of Gary's life, from friends and neigbours to the portfolio manager that dealt with his investments to show that Gary was not only sane, but he was also shrewd, with a level of intelligence so high that he could easily fake the insanity that he was now purporting had caused his offences. Without that insanity defense, Gary really had nothing to work with. He tried to shift the blame for the killings to the other women in the basement, claiming that they'd killed Sandy for being a lesbian and that Josefina had been behind the death of Debbie. He further asserted that he'd merely signed the confession along with her as he felt partially to blame for putting the women in that situation to start with. In the midst of an incomparable media frenzy, he went to trial in 1988 and was found guilty of all charges. Two counts of first-degree murder, six counts of kidnapping, five counts of rape, four counts of aggravated assault, and two counts of involuntary deviant sexual intercourse. He was sentenced to death for his crimes and transferred to the State Correctional Institution in Pittsburgh, where he would remain for the rest of his days.

After one year in prison, he made another suicide attempt, hoarding the Thorazine tablets prescribed for his mental health issues until he believed he had a lethal dose and then taking them all at once. This too was unsuccessful.

As the date of his execution slowly crept closer, Gary instructed his lawyers that he no longer wished to appeal the decision that had been made. He still claimed that he was innocent, despite all evidence to the contrary, but he believed that if the state executed an innocent man, then it might bring about the end of the cruel practice of capital punishment. Of all the people in the world that the anti-capital punishment crowd might have allied themselves with, he was definitely the least appealing, given his history. He remained intelligent and astute in his communications, clearly recognizing that while his own case was unwinnable if he could somehow influence the political climate to result in the outlawing of execution, then he might yet survive. This grand scheme, like all his others, was met with abject failure.

At what must have seemed like the very last moment, two unexpected saviors arrived, campaigning to have a stay of execution granted on the basis that Gary was not mentally competent to waive his right to appeal. Those saviors; his ex-wife Betty, and his daughter with Anjeanette Davidson; Maxine, who had grown up in care and was now of an age where she could make her voice heard in the case of her father.

Neither of these attempts were successful either, so the apparatus of the state kept grinding on towards its inevitable end. Two slices of cheese pizza and a cup of black coffee served as Gary's last meal, and on the 6th of July 1999, he was executed by lethal injection at the Rockview State Correctional Institute in Bellefonte, Pennsylvania before his body was cremated and the ashes scattered in an undisclosed location.

He would be one of only three people executed in Pennsylvania since it became legal again in 1976, and the last to die there by the hand of the state at the time of this book's publication.

Gary Heidnik's ultimate goal may have been to leave a lasting legacy through children, though none of his biological children carry his name, but even in failing to achieve that goal, he did leave behind a testament to the cruelty that man is capable of when convinced of his superiority over everyone else. A legacy that would be memorialized not only in works of True Crime but also in fiction. He served as one of the inspirations for the character of Buffalo Bill in the film, *The Silence of the Lambs,* and songs have been written about him and his crimes. He will be remembered, not as a genius who founded an empire spanning until the end of time, but as a monster. A cruel and petty man who was so obsessed with his legacy that he destroyed it before it could even be built. All that Gary Heidnik has become in history is a footnote about the horrors that people inflict on one another. A nightmare haunting the collective unconscious of every woman walking down a dark street at night alone. He ultimately had every advantage in life and chose to use those advantages to prey on society's most vulnerable. Disguising himself as a holy man as he raped the mentally disabled black women that he encountered.

He was an egomaniac, so convinced of his own self-worth and importance that it granted him free rein to do anything that he pleased. He was the most important person in the world, the only real person in the world, while those around him were merely toys or tools to be used. From his beginnings with boundless potential to make the world a better place, he instead chose time and time again to make it worse. To aggrandize himself above all else, regardless of the cost. He made money by bilking the poorest in society out of theirs. He gained power by finding the most vulnerable communities and setting himself up as their leader. He gained love, or at least what he thought of as love, by chaining up strangers in his basement, torturing them, raping them, and ruining their lives. Whatever cruelty any other person would have shied away from, he performed. Whatever morals held back other people from doing as he did, he clearly did not embrace. He was a monster in the truest sense of the word, completely devoid of all the positive attributes of humanity, turning all of his boundless potential into a hideous monument to himself. With his intelligence, he could have cured diseases and solved problems that most people can't even contend with on an intellectual level, but instead, he chose to lie, cheat, steal, rape and murder.

He paid the ultimate price for his crimes, and suffered the worst punishment that society could dole out, yet somehow, it feels as though the books still were not balanced. Gary Heidnik took and took and took. He took from everyone he ever met; he took everything that he could get. Small wonder that his legacy ended up being a deficit.

THE PIT

Want More?

Did you enjoy *The Pit* and want some more True Crime?

YOUR FREE BOOK IS WAITING

From bestselling author Ryan Green

There is a man who is officially classed as "**Britain's most dangerous prisoner**"

The man's name is Robert Maudsley, and his crimes earned him the nickname "**Hannibal the Cannibal**"

This free book is an exploration of his story...

amazonkindle   nook   kobo   iBooks

★★★★★ *"Ryan brings the horrifying details to life. I can't wait to read more by this author!"*

Get a free copy of **Robert Maudsley: Hannibal the Cannibal** when you sign up to join my Reader's Group.

www.ryangreenbooks.com/free-book

Every Review Helps

If you enjoyed the book and have a moment to spare, I would really appreciate a short review on Amazon. Your help in spreading the word is gratefully received and reviews make a huge difference to helping new readers find me. Without reviewers, us self-published authors would have a hard time!

Type in your link below to be taken straight to my book review page.

US   geni.us/pitUS

UK   geni.us/pitUK

Australia geni.us/pitAUS

Canada   geni.us/pitCA

Thank you! I can't wait to read your thoughts.

About Ryan Green

Ryan Green is a true crime author who lives in Herefordshire, England with his wife, three children, and two dogs. Outside of writing and spending time with his family, Ryan enjoys walking, reading and windsurfing.

Ryan is fascinated with History, Psychology and True Crime. In 2015, he finally started researching and writing his own work and at the end of the year, he released his first book on Britain's most notorious serial killer, Harold Shipman.

He has since written several books on lesser-known subjects, and taken the unique approach of writing from the killer's perspective. He narrates some of the most chilling scenes you'll encounter in the True Crime genre.

You can sign up to Ryan's newsletter to receive a free book, updates, and the latest releases at:

WWW.RYANGREENBOOKS.COM

More Books by Ryan Green

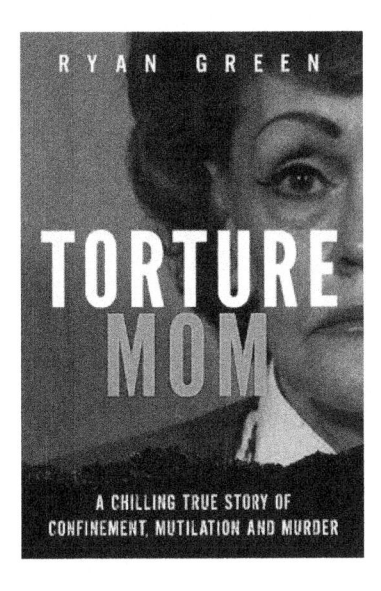

In July 1965, teenagers Sylvia and Jenny Likens were left in the temporary care of Gertrude Baniszewski, a middle-aged single mother and her seven children.

The Baniszewski household was overrun with children. There were few rules and ample freedom. Sadly, the environment created a dangerous hierarchy of social Darwinism where the strong preyed on the weak.

What transpired in the following three months was both riveting and chilling. The case shocked the entire nation and would later be described as "The single worst crime perpetuated against an individual in Indiana's history".

More Books by Ryan Green

On 29th February 2000, John Price took out a restraining order against his girlfriend, Katherine Knight. Later that day, he told his co-workers that she had stabbed him and if he were ever to go missing, it was because Knight had killed him.

The next day, Price didn't show up for work.

A co-worker was sent to check on him. They found a bloody handprint by the front door and they immediately contacted the police. The local police force was not prepared for the chilling scene they were about to encounter.

Price's body was found in a chair, legs crossed, with a bottle of lemonade under his arm. He'd been decapitated and skinned. The "skin-suit" was hanging from a meat hook in the living room and his head was found in the kitchen, in a pot of vegetables that was still warm. There were two plates on the dining table, each had the name of one of Price's children on it. She was attempting to serve his body parts to his children.

More Books by Ryan Green

In 1944, as the Nazis occupied Paris, the French Police and Fire Brigade were called to investigate a vile-smelling smoke pouring out from a Parisian home. Inside, they were confronted with a scene from a nightmare. They found a factory line of bodies and multiple furnaces stocked with human remains.

When questioned, Dr. Petiot claimed that he was a part of the Resistance and the bodies they discovered belonged to Nazi collaborators that he killed for the cause. The French Police, resentful of Nazi occupation and confused by a rational alternative, allowed him to leave.

Was the respected Doctor a clandestine hero fighting for national liberty or a deviant using dire domestic circumstances to his advantage? One thing is for certain, the Police and the Nazis both wanted to get their hands on Dr. Marcel Petiot to find out the truth.

More Books by Ryan Green

In 1861, the police of a rural French village tore their way into the woodside home of Martin Dumollard. Inside, they found chaos. Paths had been carved through mounds of bloodstained clothing, reaching as high as the ceiling in some places.

The officers assumed that the mysterious maid-robber had killed one woman but failed in his other attempts. Yet, it was becoming sickeningly clear that there was a vast gulf between the crimes they were aware of and the ones that had truly been committed.

Would Dumollard's wife expose his dark secret or was she inextricably linked to the atrocities? Whatever the circumstances, everyone was desperate to discover whether the bloody garments belonged to some of the 648 missing women.

Stay in the loop with the latest releases and exclusive offers by following Ryan!

Follow me:

Facebook geni.us/ryangreenFB

Instagram geni.us/ryangreenIG

Amazon geni.us/ryangreenAM

www.ryangreenbooks.com

RYAN GREEN

Free True Crime Audiobook

Sign up to Audible and use your free credit to download this collection of twelve books. If you cancel within 30 days, there's no charge!

WWW.RYANGREENBOOKS.COM/FREE-AUDIOBOOK

"Ryan Green has produced another excellent book and belongs at the top with true crime writers such as M. William Phelps, Gregg Olsen and Ann Rule" –**B.S. Reid**

"Wow! Chilling, shocking and totally riveting! I'm not going to sleep well after listening to this but the narration was fantastic. Crazy story but highly recommend for any true crime lover!" –**Mandy**

"Torture Mom by Ryan Green left me pretty speechless. The fact that it's a true story is just...wow" –**JStep**

"Graphic, upsetting, but superbly read and written" –**Ray C**

WWW.RYANGREENBOOKS.COM/FREE-AUDIOBOOK

Printed in Dunstable, United Kingdom